Naturalistic Evaluation

DISCARD

David D. Williams, *Editor*

NEW DIRECTIONS FOR PROGRAM EVALUATION

A Publication of the American Evaluation Association

*A joint organization of the Evaluation Research Society
and the Evaluation Network*

MARK W. LIPSEY, *Editor-in-Chief*

Number 30, June 1986

Paperback sourcebooks in
The Jossey-Bass Higher Education and
Social and Behavioral Sciences Series

Jossey-Bass Inc., Publishers
San Francisco • London

David D. Williams (Ed.).
Naturalistic Evaluation.
New Directions for Program Evaluation, no. 30.
San Francisco: Jossey-Bass, 1986.

New Directions for Program Evaluation Series
A Publication of the American Evaluation Association
Mark W. Lipsey, *Editor-in-Chief*

New Directions for Program Evaluation (publication number USPS
449-050) is published quarterly by Jossey-Bass Inc., Publishers, and is
sponsored by the American Evaluation Association. Second-class
postage rates are paid at San Francisco, California, and at
additional mailing offices.

Correspondence:
Subscriptions, single-issue orders, change of address notices,
undelivered copies, and other correspondence should be sent to
Subscriptions, Jossey-Bass Inc., Publishers, 433 California Street,
San Francisco, California 94104.

Editorial correspondence should be sent to the Editor-in-Chief,
Mark Lipsey, Psychology Department, Claremont Graduate School,
Claremont, Calif. 91711.

Library of Congress Catalog Card Number 85-8189S

International Standard Serial Number ISSN 0164-7989

International Standard Book Number ISBN 87589-728-2

Cover art by WILLI BAUM

Manufactured in the United States of America

Ordering Information

The paperback sourcebooks listed below are published quarterly and can be ordered either by subscription or single-copy.

Subscriptions cost $40.00 per year for institutions, agencies, and libraries. Individuals can subscribe at the special rate of $30.00 per year *if payment is by personal check.* (Note that the full rate of $40.00 applies if payment is by institutional check, even if the subscription is designated for an individual.) Standing orders are accepted.

Single copies are available at $9.95 when payment accompanies order, and *all single-copy orders under $25.00 must include payment.* (California, New Jersey, New York, and Washington, D.C., residents please include appropriate sales tax.) For billed orders, cost per copy is $9.95 plus postage and handling. (Prices subject to change without notice.)

Bulk orders (ten or more copies) of any individual sourcebook are available at the following discounted prices: 10-49 copies, $8.95 each; 50-100 copies, $7.96 each; over 100 copies, *inquire.* Sales tax and postage and handling charges apply as for single copy orders.

To ensure correct and prompt delivery, all orders must give either the *name of an individual* or an *official purchase order number.* Please submit your order as follows:

Subscriptions: specify series and year subscription is to begin.
Single Copies: specify sourcebook code (such as, PE1) and first two words of title.

Mail orders for United States and Possessions, Latin America, Canada, Japan, Australia, and New Zealand to:
Jossey-Bass Inc., Publishers
433 California Street
San Francisco, California 94104

Mail orders for all other parts of the world to:
Jossey-Bass Limited
28 Banner Street
London EC1Y 8QE

New Directions for Program Evaluation
Mark W. Lipsey, *Editor-in-Chief*

Contents

New Directions for Program Evaluation

A Quarterly Publication of the American Evaluation Association
(A Joint Organization of the Evaluation Research Society and
Evaluation Network)

Editor-in-Chief:

Mark W. Lipsey, Psychology, Claremont Graduate School

Editorial Advisory Board:

Scarvia B. Andersen, Psychology, Georgia Institute of Technology
Gerald L. Barkdoll, U.S. Food and Drug Administration, Washington
  D.C.
Robert F. Boruch, Psychology, Northwestern University
Timothy C. Brock, Psychology, Ohio State University
Donald T. Campbell, Social Relations, Lehigh University
Eleanor Chelimsky, U.S. General Accounting Office, Washington D.C.
James A. Ciarlo, Mental Health Systems Evaluation, University of Denver
Ross F. Conner, Social Ecology, University of California, Irvine
David S. Cordray, Psychology, Northwestern University
Robert W. Covert, Evaluation Research Center, University of Virginia
Lois-ellin Datta, U.S. General Accounting Office, Washington D.C.
Barbara Gross Davis, Educational Development, University of California,
  Berkeley
Howard E. Freeman, Sociology, University of California, Los Angeles
Egon G. Guba, Education, Indiana University
Edward S. Halpern, AT&T Bell Laboratories, Naperville, Illinois
Harry P. Hatry, The Urban Institute, Washington D.C.
Michael Hendricks, MH Associates, Washington D.C.
Gary T. Henry, Joint Legislative Audit and Review Commission, Virginia
Dennis H. Holmes, Education, George Washington University
Ernest R. House, CIRCE, University of Illinois, Urbana-Champaign
Jeanette M. Jerrell, Cognos Associates, Los Altos, California
Karen E. Kirkhart, Educational Psychology, University of Texas, Austin
Henry M. Levin, Education, Stanford University
Richard J. Light, Government, Harvard University
Charles McClintock, Human Service Studies, Cornell University
William A. McConnell, San Francisco Community Mental Health
  Programs
Jeri Nowakowski, Leadership & Educ. Policy Studies, Northern Illinois
  University
Michael Q. Patton, International Programs, University of Minnesota
Charles S. Reichardt, Psychology, University of Denver

American Evaluation Association, 9555 Persimmon Tree Road, Potomac, MD 20854

Editor's Notes

Traditionally, the purposes and procedures of naturalistic inquiry and program evaluation have been divergent. Identified by a variety of labels (such as qualitative research, ethnography, participant observation, and fieldwork), naturalistic inquiry evolved through anthropology, sociology, and other disciplines as a way of "understanding" people and the meaning behind their activities. The focus of naturalistic inquiry is on describing human processes and using the views of the participants being studied to guide the generation of hypotheses and the development of theories about those processes. Naturalistic inquirers usually view the people under study as collaborators in this discovery process. The inquiry procedures are meant to be nonjudgmental, with relatively more emphasis on the processes by which outcomes are produced than on outcomes or products. Inquiry focuses on processes occurring naturally, without manipulation of variables by the inquirer.

Systematic program evaluation has evolved from informal evaluation casually made by all people to a formal means of estimating the merit of processes and products (evaluands). The focus is usually on defining the criteria of value for a given study, collecting data on the activities and objects of interest, and comparing the activities and achievements to the criteria to assess the value of the evaluand. Although clear descriptions of the criteria and the products and processes to be calculated are essential, the emphasis is on using those descriptions to make value judgments rather than to "understand" participants' meanings or to generate hypotheses and theories to explain participants' actions. Generally, the results of evaluations are intended for the immediate practical use of policy makers, product developers, and consumers.

In spite of differences in purpose between naturalistic inquiry and systematic evaluation, several evaluation theorists (see for example, Guba and Lincoln, 1981; Patton, 1980; and Stake, 1975, who are cited in Chapter Six) have suggested that the naturalistic approach be used as an alternative paradigm for guiding evaluators. They contrast the data collection techniques of ethnographers and participant observers with those of experimenters, expert witnesses, and opinion pollers to argue that the qualitative perspective, defensibly obtained, can radically improve many evaluation efforts. More and more evaluators have begun to explore the naturalistic approach to see if and how it may be applied effectively in a variety of settings. Some have attempted evaluations that are exclusively naturalistic (including no quantitative methods) while others have combined naturalistic components (such as participant observations and repeated informal interviews) with more traditional tests, questionnaires, and structured interviews to create mixed-method studies.

The contributors to this sourcebook represent both the theorists who advocate naturalistic approaches to evaluation and the practitioners who conduct naturalistic evaluations. Analyses of their experiences, as presented in the following chapters, should aid other evaluators and recipients of evaluations (such as clients, participants in programs that are evaluated, and students of evaluation) in understanding how naturalistic methods and evaluation purposes complement and conflict with one another.

In Chapter One Hébert provides a contextually rich example of what naturalistic evaluation is. In Chapter Two, through the use of examples from several recent evaluations, Fetterman highlights possible solutions to tensions and conflicts between the naturalistic paradigm and the needs of evaluation. M. Smith argues in Chapter Three for blending both qualitative and quantitative methods, when appropriate, in naturalistic evaluations. In Chapter Four, L. Smith and Kleine propose the triangulation of three modes of qualitative inquiry to enhance systematic evaluation: participant observation, life story interviews, and historical analysis. Lincoln and Guba present Chapter Five to expand their earlier thinking and outline precautions evaluators should take to make their naturalistic evaluations rigorous. As a conclusion to the collection, Williams suggests in Chapter Six means by which an evaluator or an evaluation client can decide if a naturalistic approach or component is most appropriate for a given evaluation situation. Finally, based on their experience in preparing naturalistic inquirers, Biklen and Bogdan introduce additional readings in Chapter Seven that may assist students, practitioners, and evaluation recipients in learning to conduct and critique naturalistic evaluations.

David D. Williams
Editor

David D. Williams is assistant professor of curriculum and instructional science at Brigham Young University, specializing in research on evaluation.

*Permeated with ethical and political concerns, with
racial, gender, and cultural differences, this case study
deals with the specifics of Native American education
in Canada. It is an example of educational change and
takes its larger meaning from that reality.*

Naturalistic Evaluation in Practice: A Case Study

Yvonne M. Hébert

What is naturalistic evaluation in practice? Naturalistic evaluation is a
process by which evaluators seek to know and understand an evaluand,
then to present their knowledge and understanding to others. This process
may be difficult and painful; it may be gentle and joyful. It involves,
however, the act of describing and judging, as does any other evaluation
method. The difference lies in how the description and judgment are
achieved and rendered. The generalizations that result from naturalistic
evaluation are arrived at by "recognizing the similarities of objects and
issues in and out of context and by sensing the natural covariations of
happenings" (Stake, 1978, p. 6). Hence, naturalistic evaluation in practice
aims at understanding, at extending experience, and at increasing a conviction in that which is known.

I wish to thank those around me for discussion of the many issues arising
out of this study: my fellow evaluators on the team; Orrison Burgess (Regina);
Claire Goldsmith (Calgary); Margaret Lipp (Regina); Art Schwartz (Calgary); and
especially Don McCaskill (Peterborough) and Bob Stake (Champaign) who have
repeatedly encouraged me to write this up. I also wish to thank the people of
Region A/B for the opportunity to learn and to grow.

D. D. Williams (Ed.). *Naturalistic Evaluation.*
New Directions for Program Evaluation, no. 30. San Francisco: Jossey-Bass, June 1986.

3

The purpose of this chapter is to provide an account of a naturalistic evaluation undertaken in the early 1980s in the culturally rich Canadian province of British Columbia. The evaluation examined innovative programming in Native American education, centering on languages and cultures in two adjacent school districts and consisted of a postmortem in one district and a needs assessment in the other district. The account is told from the perspective that comes from a year-long period of reflection. Essentially one person's views and experience, the telling is assisted with specifics from files, telephone notes, audiotapes, and interview notes.

This narrative is structured around three major issues that emerged from this experience. The first issue, which deals with determining the boundaries of the inquiry, weaves itself throughout the study, from the time of contract negotiation through to the final reporting. The second issue deals with establishing the realities of the programs under evaluation and of the study itself by focusing on interactional and communication events between stakeholders and evaluators. The third focuses on the experiential learning that occurred through introspection and reflection as a result of this evaluation study. Examples from the case study are written in the style of a personal journal.

Boundaries

The boundaries of the inquiry were established and re-established throughout the evaluation process by its context, in the contract negotiations, during data collection, in a threat to completion, and through reporting. Bounding the inquiry involved identifying the evaluation's organizational issues, setting limits on its scope, and distinguishing personal style, power, and politics from relevant matters of principle.

Context. This evaluation study was mounted within the broad context of Indian self-determination. In 1972 the National Indian Brotherhood put forward a policy paper calling for Indian Control of Indian Education, and proposing two underlying principles: parental responsibility and local control of education. Since then, Canada has been the scene of an overt struggle as aboriginal peoples have sought to gain control of all aspects of the education of their young: policy and budget control, deployment of human and material resources, curriculum content, and school organization. Although education in Canada is a provincial matter, the responsibility and control of Indian education has been lodged in the federal government through legal and parliamentary documents (Longboat, 1986). Educational services are dispensed in day schools increasingly operated by Indian tribes since the mid 1970s, in a few remaining residential schools, and through federal-provincial agreements known as Master Tuition Agreements, which transfer monies per Indian student to provincial departments of education and on to school districts (see Barman and others, 1986, for further discussion).

Both the clients initiating the evaluation and the evaluators perceived and accepted the need for innovations with respect to the education of Indian students. Moreover, both accepted the two underlying principles of Indian education. The client-initiators of the evaluation study spearheaded and administered the innovations, each in their respective provincial school districts. In School District A, the client-initiator was coordinator of an administrative unit exclusively for Indian education progams. This unit, the Native Indian Education Division, was linked in practice directly to the superintendency as chief educational officer, bypassing other administrative levels, including assistant superintendents. In School District B, the client-initiator was an assistant superintendent, also bearing the title of director of Indian education, with recent responsibility for Indian education in addition to other duties.

The context further limited the study. The maintenance of the aboriginal languages is linked to the ethnovitality of the cultural groups (Giles and others, 1977), since the languages express the groups' identity and cohesion (Smolicz, 1979). Languages and their role in educational endeavors frequently become rallying points for internal collective revitalization efforts of devalued and dominated peoples who strive actively to reverse economic, social, and political power relations in their favor (Hamers and Blanc, 1983). Thus, an evaluation study of Indian language programs was central to Indian education.

This evaluation study occurred in Canada's westernmost province and involved four distinct languages and some of their dialects. Two of the languages were migrant to the region, one more recently than the other. The cultural identities of the aboriginal people involved were linked primarily to the dialect grouping (Hébert, 1984). Being located within the same culture area, the study's stakeholding aboriginal peoples were similar in very general cultural traits, but with significant cultural distinctions (Driver, 1969).

Contracting. The major issue in this particular context was to determine whether the public school system was the appropriate agency to have responsibility for Indian language education. The emergence of this issue occurred in four identifiable stages, as illustrated by journal extracts: (1) in the initial contact, (2) in the subsequent negotiations, (3) in an intervening period of reflection, and (4) in the contract negotiations.

1. The Initial Contact.

It is early morning on May 18, and I have just returned home late last night from fieldwork in northern British Columbia schools. The phone rings. It is the coordinator of Indian education in School District A, who has been trying to reach me and is concerned about her own aboriginal peoples. "We have tried," she says, "we have tried to teach our languages in our schools; three times we have tried, but we have failed. . . . Would you be interested," she continues, "in a four-month contract as a linguistic consultant, September to December, to look at what we've been doing, to evaluate, to meet with language teachers and linguists, and to come up with a total overview of languages and recommendations by January?"

2. Subsequent Negotiations: A Meeting with Representatives from the Two School Districts and Four Members of the Evaluation Team, June 23.

The coordinator of School District A speaks and sketches the background of the region, including the development of the Indian education unit and its several successful programs. Then she focuses on the Indian languages program, telling us the number of languages, the teachers, their school assignment, and the problem—declining enrollment. The last incident had the language teacher on salary, September to December last year, for curriculum development but not teaching for lack of students. "This is a treatment belittling of the languages," she comments. She speaks of the supporting role taken by linguists in the area, of parental reaction including adverse ones, and of her view that the languages should be taught in the public schools.

The representative from School District B, sitting in for the assistant superintendent, speaks briefly of the situation in their district. They had a language program for a year, but it is now nonexistent for lack of continuous enrollment. There is considerable school board support in District B. Their policy is to start slowly and to progress systematically. A report is seen as the best way to get a language program off the ground, and they want to know the steps involved—a process type of thing. . . .

3. A Period of Reflection over the Summer.

I must prepare for this evaluation study. Although I've read a bit, I need to know more. Bob Stake is giving a course here this summer. I think I'll sit in if I can. What is the basic issue around which this study can be organized? From what's been said and what I know generally in the province, probably the issue is whether or not the native Indian languages belong in the public schools in the A/B Region.

4. In the Contract Negotiations: September 8.

We start the study today. T and I have traveled to Region A/B and have talked at length with the two representatives from school districts A and B. The terms of reference are agreed on and typed up for our four signatures, exactly as follows:

Given the A and B school districts' commitment to considering native Indian language programs in the public schools, and given the School District A's native Indian Education Council's commitment to having native Indian language programs, the evaluation team will:

1. Determine the factors which affect the implementation of these programs from onset to fall 1982, for the following languages: N, S, K, and C, examining in particular: administrative structure, policies, and practices; curriculum methods; teaching practices and training; and facilities.

2. Ascertain the community support, if any, for such school programs among Native Indian parents and teachers.

3. Consider whether the public school system is the appropriate responsible agency for native Indian language programs in the A/B region.

The problem statement in the contract further bounds the evaluation, as any inquiry can be bound, through the use of the problem statement as a limiting tool (Guba and Lincoln, 1981). However, the contract itself permitted a very broad inquiry into the context of Indian language education in the region. The interviews conducted by team members, either in pairs or singly, also broadened the topic of the inquiry.

During Data Collection. After the second field trip to the region, following open-ended semi-structured interviews with principals and some teaching staff, with the districts' two representatives and superintendents, with some community members, primarily elders at this point, and with four language teachers, it became apparent in a review of notes and audiotapes and in debriefing sessions among team members that nearly all interviews showed a similar pattern. Very early in the interviews, the respondents broadened their discussion to Indian education itself. Moreover, school-based personnel focused on the process and style of the innovations in Indian education, including the language programs in School District A, while the content of the language programs received close attention from the language instructors, and from linguists at a nearby university. Thus, the boundaries of the inquiry were being broadened by the respondents and program participants, while themes and concerns were emerging early. Attempts to verify the hypothesized patterns, developed on the basis of early interviews, yielded confirmation in subsequent interviews. Moreover, the interviewers' deliberate attempts to narrow the discussion to language education were regularly ignored or set aside.

A Threat to Completion. Midway through the study, at a meeting of the local evaluation committee, rescheduled for early December, the two evaluators reported on their findings.

> Two members from District A have not yet arrived: the coordinator and an elder. Phone calls are made by the staff at the District B offices, the location of the meeting. The elder G, a member of the Indian Education Council, is stranded at the office of Coordinator A, missing his ride with her to the meeting. Coordinator A is absent from work today and cannot be contacted. Reluctantly, we start without them. T presents our methods and our findings to date, indicating our sources of data. T follows this up with her diagram of the stakeholding groups in these two school districts. Discussion ensues and everybody present seems satisfied with the proceedings, and further inquiries are planned. I inform the members present of the interviewees' concerns about the style of the innovations in School District A, a style generally perceived as intimidation and harassment. Trustee A is taken aback, having had no idea of the extent of this and having been party to the innovations. Trustee B and Assistant Superintendent B seem to understand what is being said, and Trustee B confirms our findings with further instances, since the administrator under discussion actually resides in Region B and is well known.
>
> A few days later, Coordinator A visits Assistant Superintendent B, who has requested Trustee B's presence at the meeting. Coordinator A worries that the evaluation is getting into difficulty, since it is getting involved with community politics. The two B's fail to see any problem here and the meeting is soon over.

The boundaries of the inquiry, as expanded by the interviews, were perceived to be a problem that one stakeholding group had with the client-initiator of School District A. By January this concern threatened completion of the evaluation study:

> In early January, Coordinator A and chief political ally W, who is president of a native political association and of the Indian Education Council of District A, telephoned me long distance. Expressing concern over difficulties with the evaluation, A invites me to appear before the council to explain myself and my methods. The invitation is declined due to other commitments and the discussion heats up. I point out that the council is an advisory committee and that the contract is with the school district, that is, with the board through its representative. Coordinator A insists that the council's powers and functions are equivalent to those of the school board. In full fury, A insists: "You are getting into community pol-

itics, and only Indian people will deal with Indian politics." At this point banging my fist on my desk, I shout back: "I'm sorry I'm not Indian, but you hired me!" With steam subsiding at both ends of the telephone call, I request trust and time to finish the study. It is almost done—just one more brief field trip and the report writing can be completed for our end-of-January deadline. W agrees and A follows suit.

The invitation to appear before the council was perceived to be a diversionary tactic, very likely to result in the termination of the study, to the considerable embarrassment and concern of client B, the evaluators, the superiors of client A, and other stakeholding groups.

Bounding Through Reporting. Trying to limit the inquiry while presenting the full range of the findings, organized around the emerging themes and concerns, presented a methodological dilemma. Accepting the principles of Indian education meant to us that the findings were to be presented in an empathetic, positive, and constructive manner. Yet the concern over the process of the innovations in School District A must be included in the final written report. This was addressed by considering stages of program innovation and implementation, in which an initial stage of creating and developing programs for minority students requires much blustering, posturing, and even intimidation and harassment of a political nature, in a possibly recalcitrant and racist school system. The programs were no longer perceived by program participants as being in their initial stages. A number of school-based personnel indicated the need for sound managerial practices. Thus, the stages of the program planning and the needs of the programming had changed since the initiation of the innovations. The draft of the final report provided this analysis in tactful tones and suggested some remediation to attain the desired managerial style. The evaluators realized that the individuals concerned were likely to take a jaundiced view of the analysis. The negotiations of the final report were expected to be stormy.

In anticipation, the evaluation team was expanded for the early February meeting of the local evaluation committee to include two senior academics familiar with the study and knowledgeable in multicultural education and evaluation, in addition to the team member responsible for the questionnaire survey of the community. As we expected, local representation had changed somewhat. Coordinator A and School Trustee added Native Politician W. The elder G from District A was absent, and an elected Indian representative from District B was turned away by Coordinator A, who claimed to represent Indian people in District B as well.

The report draft was attacked by Coordinator A and Politician W on several points: the broadening of the inquiry in response to interview data; the naturalistic method in which issues, concerns, and themes emerge from collected data; the link between Indian languages and Indian education; and the sections dealing with administrative structures, policies, and practices. After much discussion and negotiation, the evaluators agreed to add a set of recommendations to the report for each school district, to soften the wording in a few instances, to color-code certain key pages, and to prepare separate executive summaries, also color-coded, so as to separate out the two school districts to prevent unintended comparisons by readers. Visibly upset, Coordinator A left the meeting quickly while Politician W shook hands and visited with the two senior evaluators.

The evaluators faced the dilemma of following a client's directives and disregarding findings and contract, or of being consistent to the method of naturalistic inquiry but facing the intense dissatisfaction of one client group. The study was completed with the final report retained in essence, subject only to minor revisions of the draft. The monies were finally collected after further negotiations with Superintendent A. The greater cause and principles of Indian education were supported with an increased intensity in conviction of the knowledge and understanding gained of the language programs, other existing native studies programs, and the importance of their context.

Establishing the Realities of the Programs

Since neither school district had an ongoing Indian language program at the time of the evaluation, the available data were limited. Using indirect means to overcome this limitation, the evaluation team set about establishing program realities with documentary evidence, interview data from program participants providing indirect program observation, and confirmation of realities from multiple written and oral sources. Additionally, attention to central interactional events salient to program participants and other stakeholders focused inquiry on those elements of cultural and social organization that were relevant to program enactment (Dorr-Bremme, 1985; Hymes, 1974; Bauman and Sherzer, 1974; Philips, 1983). These events, supported by documentary analysis, yielded rich data, serving to establish the realities of Indian language programming in these particular communities.

Finding Out the Basic Facts. Central to the evaluation are basic facts concerning the languages and their speech communities, school programming and other community language programs, the Indian education units within the school districts, the stakeholding groups, the formal and informal curriculum, and the community context. Having noticed the use of various names for the languages and vagueness with respect to program details, the evaluation teams first focused on determining the language and school program facts while organizing the community survey with a questionnaire developed by a team member and a review of formal curriculum materials to be obtained from the language instructors.

Documents provided by Coordinator A were analyzed as a first step in determining program facts. This analysis yielded discrepancies about the number of students in the language classes and the dates of program life, initial information about some of the stakeholding groups, considerable information about public relations events organized and sponsored by the Indian Education Division and Council, some information about the functioning of the council but no information about its election procedures or in support of the claim that it was the equivalent of a duly elected school board, and no budgetary or policy information. Repeated requests for the missing documentation were unsuccessful but led to additional questions to be raised in extensive interviews of school and program personnel. This in turn led us back to a re-examination of the written evidence in the form of minutes of meetings, memos, council brochures, and other file documents. Thus, the documentary evidence corroborated interview data and provided more complex levels of understanding of how social and cultural organization functioned to influence the program. This process provided material and time for reflection on possibilities, if any, of future programming in Indian languages.

We borrowed curriculum materials used and developed by F, the language teacher with greatest seniority, and transmitted them to a team member for an off-site curriculum review. This analysis occasioned interaction between the reviewer and the evaluation director about the history and use of the materials. Diplomatically critical and constructive, the reviewer's chapter in the final report was the first curricular review of Indian language materials in the province and as such provided an insider to the culture with the opportunity to set standards for Indian language education, a unique feature of the study.

Other sources were sought out to provide necessary language and school facts. Research of the linguistic and anthropological literature provided us with the specialists' names for the languages, dialects, speech communities, their geographical distribution, and their relationships. This information was corroborated with interview data from elders, a linguist closely implicated in Indian language education in the province, and an anthropological educator similarly involved. These persons also explained the shift in language names, its timing and motivation, and how it had been linked with the rising consciousness of group identity and self-determination. These interviews were also highly informative with respect to the identification and characterization of stakeholding groups, some programming details, and considerable contextual information. Other interviews were used to triangulate this information, with team members constantly seeking to corroborate data and perceptions from multiple sources while also checking their own perceptions and findings with each other.

The community household survey, which proceeded well and went according to schedule, provided facts on community context. Population lists were compiled by both school districts, with details of addresses, telephone numbers, language affiliation, and membership in tribes or other native Indian organizations. Candidates for the job of community interviewer were identified by Coordinator A, who also allocated space for R to interview, select, and train these individuals to implement the community household survey. The process of implementation yielded evaluative data, since the evaluator R and the two interviewers remained in frequent contact and participated in the double-checking of findings and perceptions. Analysis of the questionnaire results provided a description of Indian language use in the region, determined the extent of community interest and commitment, and recorded opinions on issues relating to the education of Indian children and, in particular, issues concerning the learning of Indian languages. These findings were then related to the other information gathered in the evaluation for the final meeting of the local evaluation committee and during the preparation of the final report, which included detailed descriptions, tables, and other figures.

Finally, a community meeting, organized by the administrators and staff of both school districts and located in a high school in District B, also helped establish the basic facts. Diagrams of the participants and their seating arrangements, made by several team members present at the community meeting, provided excellent information about certain stakeholding groups, their interests, and points of view. The discussion revealed some of the factionalism associated with these stakeholding groups, as can be illustrated with two points of controversy: one dealing with the choice of language to be taught in District B, the other with the choice of orthography. Many of those present wanted only the ancestral language of the area taught in the schools. Other stakeholders who wanted the migrant language taught as well were largely absent from the meeting, since they perceived the event as being a stacked or closed meeting.

The orthography controversy also surfaced at the community meeting, with elder D, who figures eminently in Indian language education in the area, eschewing the orthography developed by a local university linguist for the ancestral language, preferring his own. In so doing, he disassociated himself from all those involved with this linguist. The details of this disassociation were revealed in interviews conducted well after the community meeting. The disassociation included the elder's own brother who had studied linguistics at the nearby university. Now deceased, his brother's language materials lie dormant, in the hands of his heirs, with considerable resentment on both sides of the family, extending into the community. Meanwhile, the elder, with his strongly held views, continued to work and to train language teachers in the tribe-operated school, in his own orthography, pedagogical, and curricular approaches, disallowing his language teachers access to university studies. This elder D also worked with a curriculum developer in District B on native studies courses at the secondary level. In addition, D maintained his link with his niece, Coordinator A, although there was a feuding relationship between the administrator in the tribal school and Coordinator A. Significantly, the language teachers exercised considerable caution in meeting with the university-based evaluators, arranging the visit during the absence of both the elder and their administrator, which permitted a bi-directional flow of information.

The impact of this factionalism was revealed in many sources of data, both oral and written, converging on the facts central to the evaluation. Given the conflicts between the leading educational figures of the area, meetings between them tended not to occur, with a concomitant lack of consensus with respect to directions for Indian education in this region. Additionally, representation and participation in any Indian educational endeavour in the region were subject to factionalism of this type, which permeated the entire fabric of the communities. And importantly for the children, students are enrolled or not in school programs in accordance with the ways members of these communities align themselves according to dialect group, family, and particular powerful individuals.

Indirect Program Observation. Interviews with language teachers who were asked to describe their teaching practice, their courses, and their experience provided an indirect means of program observation. The resulting descriptions were consistent in detail and in substance from one language teacher to the next, revealing their dedication and their knowledge of their subject and providing firm information on the number of students, languages, dates, and locations of public school programs. An excerpt from interview notes taken while interacting with F, the language teacher of greatest seniority in School District A, illustrates the technique:

> October 17. Comfortable in the kitchen of her home, F quietly tells us of how she got involved with teaching. The classroom was a huge room for native studies, sectioned off in three parts: one for the other language class at the far end, N's office in the middle, and F's class at one end. "The language classes didn't disturb each other. We just sat around a table at our end."
>
> "When I first got hired, a linguist from the university visited my class a couple of times." In the first year, the principal just wandered through there, without making any suggestions. "He wanted to see my program. The atmosphere between me and the kids was very good. I didn't have to discipline: good atmosphere . . . no picking on kids." He was very open to suggestions and was supportive. "I could drop in if I needed to talk to him."
>
> "I would talk in English for about five minutes before the lesson, then I would use my language, with no English translation at all. I used pictures for mostly everything." F brings out her own

extensive files and loose-leaf books, which constituted the language curriculum, and walks us through her work with much discussion of the materials and their use. "One way I learned to write in my language was to rewrite the Boas stories, so I learned the various writing systems."

She feels successful in her teaching and in motivating the kids in junior high schools. With the change to grade 2, there weren't enough kids to start a class. When she got laid off, "a guy delivered a letter directly to me. Nobody talked to me." F is tired of resting now; she is willing to work but does not see herself as a leader. She wants to know how all this turns out.

In this open-ended interaction with F, the events seen as central to her program effort were readily and reliably identified to the evaluators. Confirmation of her categories of events and her perceptions were obtained from other program participants: principals, language teachers, and other Indian teachers.

Similarly, several interviews served to illuminate indirectly the demise scenario of the school program in District A one autumn. Coordinator A waited for the principal to report on the enrollment; the principal waited for the coordinator to organize the enrollment; and the language teacher, who had prepared curriculum materials under contract over the summer, waited for notification from either that her classes awaited her. This non-deliberate, benign neglect was due to inadequate preplanning and coordination following an administrative decision to move the language program from the junior high school to two elementary schools, at the grade 2 level, in order to reach the children at an early age.

In the context of this lack of success was a past struggle between the coordinator and the principals over the control of the Indian education programs, one that the previous superintendent had resolved personally in favor of the coordinator in view of the importance of Indian control of Indian education.

Interaction and Communication

Interactional events central to the study included telephone conversations, meetings of the local evaluation committee, a community meeting, informal home visits, and office visits, especially those to school district offices, local tribal and regional tribal council offices, and community service agencies. Three interactional characteristics emerged as important to this inquiry: bartering, cross-cultural communication styles, and absence of access to clearly identifiable stakeholders. Bartering of knowledge occurred in several instances. All yielded further access to data and involved Indian individuals with either of two evaluators.

Bartering. The implementation of R's questionnaire for the community survey was carried out by two native residents of Region A/B. In continuous contact with each other over the five-month period, R provided training and information on survey techniques, including sampling procedures. This led to a return of information in the form of both volunteered tips on whom to interview in the communities and insider perspectives of the communities, which served to illuminate the evaluators and to confirm insights. This type of bartering of knowledge was not deliberate on R's part but characteristic of his general openness.

In other instances, the bartering was deliberate. Both types, however, were consistent with traditional cultural interaction patterns in this region in that the extraction of information through direct questioning was considered a violation of sociolinguistic patterns. Information was to be exchanged more indirectly. For example, a morning visit to the tribal-operated school with the two practicing language teachers began, after appropriate civilities, with a lengthy discussion of technical aspects of the Indian languages of this region. The evaluator established credibility through active participation in this exchange of knowledge. This led to acceptance of the evaluator and to a generous sharing of program information and of the program realities from the participants' point of view. This exchange was repeated but less extensively in four other instances involving language instructors and one evaluator.

Two other significant instances of bartering occurred but in reverse order, with information requested by the evaluator provided first and information requested thereafter of the evaluator. Both cases involved young tribal-office staff who wanted information on a forthcoming conference on native Indian language education. One provided information on the return travels of two language teachers, leading to interviews. The other participated in an interview on language education on his reserve.

Cross-Cultural Communication Styles. Important throughout the study, these served first, to establish credibility; second, to gain access to stakeholders; third, to understand what was being said and its style; and finally, to understand when accepted sociolinguistic styles of interaction were being violated and why. The first is best illustrated by an evening-long interview with G and his wife in their home on reserve in Region B.

> An articulate, knowledgeable, self-assured, and highly intelligent young man, G extended welcoming hospitality and gradually entered into an active discussion with the two evaluators, T and myself, permitting notes to be taken. Later on, feeling uncomfortable, he remarked that he had a friend who seemed to be writing down everything he said, but was actually writing down what he wanted G to be saying. Shortly thereafter, I put down my pen, and the discussion continued quite openly. With great confidence, G

explained his philosophy and practice of community development, setting aside any possible questions or criticisms. Much later, I countered by relating a case of an Indian community that sought outside expert help on educational matters. The consultants, appearing very confident and self-assured, were accepted and their advice applied, much to the detriment of the school situation. The outside experts had no knowledge of tribal schools or of Indian communities. Eyes widening, G talked of other things and gradually became more relaxed and open. The discussion continued until the middle of the night. Upon taking leave, G asked me to write to the grandparents of a foster child placed in his home to convey the reassuring news that the child was well looked after during his stay there. I agreed to do so, since I had met the grandparents on a previous trip to a distant comunity. G walked us to our car and asked us to let him know the next time we went to a meeting—he'd like to come and learn something!

This long interview revealed the interrelatedness of bartering and interactional styles. It mixed direct questioning with the traditional indirect and interwoven communication style of meetings that operate within a politeness system designed to save face in a non-confrontational manner (Scollon and Scollon, 1981; Philips, 1983). This successful evening led to entry into a set of previously blocked stakeholders: the elected chiefs of the reserves in Region B and the home area of the coordinator in School District A. The blockage and the gained access assisted in identifying the complexities of the serious and long-term factionalism in these particular communities.

One community meeting was organized by the client-initiators to provide input into the evaluation study. The meeting mixed communication styles from two cultures: the Indian and non-Indian. The indirectness and delayed interweaving were typical of Indian meetings, which required excellent listening skills and a good memory (Philips, 1976, 1982). Familiarity with these speech patterns was necessary to understand the substance and style of what was being said.

That Monday evening a community meeting is held at one of the secondary schools in School District B. Twenty-five people attend, including the S language teachers at the tribal school, school district staff, community members, and Coordinator A. We assist people in coming together in a large circle, rearranging tables and chairs as needed. During the discussion, we jot down the names of all those present, in their seating arrangement. The discussion ranges freely—there is no fixed agenda. Speakers do not necessarily address the same topic in sequence with other speakers. Several topics weave in and out of the meeting: choice of orthography, number of homes surveyed, optimal age to teach children a second language, the system of teaching, Indian-white relations, intense necessity of teaching Indian languages to Indian children, and which language: C or S. There is a very serious concern with sampling techniques. What if we sample the wrong ones? A comment made by a community member sits uncomfortably over the meeting: A person is not Indian if he or she doesn't speak Indian.

After the exhausting meeting, we debrief. R feels he failed to convince anybody of the value or soundness of sampling techniques. What if we pick the wrong ones? The phrase resounds in our memories. R laughs and worries. He shakes his head and good naturedly ponders the issue. Later on, we confirm that the attendance represented only some groups in the community. Much later, we come to realize that surveys and samplings are inconsistent with the group consensus mode of decision making typical of many Indian cultures, including this one. Moreover, we have no adequate way of weighing the wisdom of the elders in survey research.

Awareness of traditional communication styles obliged the evaluators to adjust themselves accordingly to avoid violations. For example, pause length between utterances, as well as control of topic, are culturally variable (Scollon and Scollon, 1981; Philips, 1976).

I must remember to pause longer when talking with A. She'll think I'm rude and I should know better. I keep interrupting her, because I start talking, thinking she has finished but she keeps on talking—her turn isn't over. I should wait a bit longer, then I'll know who's to have the floor.

Two violations of traditional sociolinguistic patterns of interaction and communication occurred: one minor and one major. The minor one, which involved a direct reprimand of myself from Coordinator A in front of T, was indicative of the possible marginality of an individual within the traditional Indian cultural group of Region A/B and of that person's position-based social status. The major violation occurred well into fieldwork, in mid-November, when one team member was unceremoniously turned away from a tribal-operated school by the administrator. This followed an interview in which the administrator had challengingly received the evaluator but had explained the prehistoric sources of factionalism in the regional communities and had given his perspective of School District B's recent attempts at consultation. He also loaned his only copy of the just-released "Indian Self-Government in Canada" (1984) for input into the evaluation.

The subsequent ejection confirmed the following: (1) the lines of the factionalism in the communities, since the evaluators were perceived as having been sent by Coordinator A although this was in Region B; (2) use of appropriate cross-cultural communication styles was essential— the team member had struck the posture of an expert coming in to help, having only skimmed the report, whereas the low-key give-and-take of knowledge bartering should have been used; and (3) I could not send inexperienced staff into what proved to be difficult field situations. As a result, the team member was extremely angry. He was withdrawn from the field, much to his consternation, and friendships were lost. This incident left me pondering how one trains and sensitizes others to do ethnographic fieldwork in cross-cultural situations, although this sort of training was not on the agenda of the evaluation team.

Absence of Access. The absence of access to clearly identifiable stakeholders was also significant in terms of establishing the realities of contextual factors influencing program enactment. One absence of access to Indian teachers and aides in School District A was overcome by a team member T early in the field work in a conversation with a teacher at her school. As part of the preliminaries of an interview, T informed her that the school district had commissioned the study and I directed it. The response opened access: "Well, why didn't you say Yvonne sent you?!" Recalling that she and I had met casually in a cafe conversation summers before while each traveling in the interior, the teacher talked at length with the evaluator although without notes or recording so as to protect the respondent. This opening led to others in the school system for T to pursue.

Another absence of access remained partially closed throughout the study in spite of my persistent attempts to interact. One of the languages in School District A was reserve-based locally, and the study needed input from elected chiefs, councilors, language instructors, and elders from that locality. The latter two groups were located, and they agreed to interviews. I was warmly received and again bartered knowledge and sources of information as indirectly requested of me. The interaction style was gentle and sad because the languages are dying out, but joyous in visits between old friends: "I wondered what happened to you! What's your news?" However, the elected community representatives were unavailable for interviews from the tribes in Region A and the regional tribal councils. The reason came over the telephone from the wife of a tribal administrator as she explained to me that he would not talk with me because Coordinator A sent me. Documentary analysis later revealed that no one from this group of stakeholders held office in the Native Indian Educational Council of School District A. Thus, even the lack of access and its interactional style provided rich data of political, social, and cultural organization affecting educational programming.

Introspection and Reflection

The experiential learning that occurred as part of this study centered on the clarification of my allegiances, responsibilities, truths, fairness, bias, and feelings, while seeking to attain the essence of naturalistic evaluation. The questions of evaluator allegiance responsibility, and fairness emerged by the second month of fieldwork, with the return of two fieldworkers. One in particular recounted gleefully the antagonism with which principals and other school-based personnel in Distract A held a certain individual. These team members identified with the school personnel whose background and experience matched those of the evaluators. To whom did we owe our allegiance? What was our responsibility and to which of the stakeholders? How were we to be fair to everyone, including those who were intensely disliked?

How were we to report these findings? Team members agreed that the evaluators owed a factual report to the boards of trustees and, if requested, an accounting of monies expended. The team did not agree on the question of allegiance. Two members with a background in educational administration felt we owed our allegiance to the boards. No one felt any particular allegiance to Coordinator A and Politician W. With my background in community-based linguistic fieldwork, I felt that we owed our allegiance to the elders and to the language program participants, especially to the language teachers. The two senior evaluators leaned toward the communities as the important bases for educational development. The matter of evaluator's allegiance was not resolved as such, although the bias toward the communities and language program participants was apparent in the final report.

Our responsibility to be fair to all concerned overrode the matter of allegiance. Being fair to someone who is perceived as seeking to control the study, the data, analysis, and conclusions, in an aggressive, emotional, and crisis-oriented manner, was rather difficult. Principles of fairness for evaluation practice proposed by House (1980) were useful for reflection by team members, including myself, but were naive in this highly politicized context; adherence cannot be coerced. Four coping strategies were employed. First, an analytic strategy permitted the evaluators to focus on the role and style of innovation in education and particularly in minority and aboriginal education, juxtaposed with stages in programming. Second, a grounding strategy enabled me to spend more fieldwork time with traditional Indian community members, rather than in the close environs of any one difficult individual. Third, humor was also used as a coping strategy; for example, we referred to one person as "Our Lady of Perpetual Hindrance." Fourth, a spiritual and emotional coping strategy of meditation quieted and calmed my feelings and thoughts so that I had the strength to continue seeing the principles and greater cause at stake and to complete the task.

Closely linked to responsibility, allegiance, fairness, and bias was establishing what and where truth was in such complexity. First of all, we realized that there were many truths. Where there were patterns of co-occurence in perspectives, in phenomena, and in insight, we looked for composite truths. But were these to be equally valued and weighed? Among these composite truths, we looked for explanatory power, which we realized was not necessarily linked to political power, to majority vote, or vested in organizational structure. This led to the wisdom expressed by the elders, to a valuing of their insight, and to the subsequent weighing of the study. Furthermore, we realized that in a factionalized situation truth was likely to be discontinuous rather than continuous, leaving us with gaps in our knowledge and understanding. This we had to accept, as well as the factionalism as part of the interrelated complexities and not as a sole characteristic of this particular community or as the sole property of aboriginal communities or cultural groups.

We also realized that truths were conditioned by what was culturally right and responsible. These were cultural groups in which group rights override individual rights and in which individualism is not highly prized. Individuals perceived as being too powerful in negative ways were subject to the sanctions of the groups, which provided some explanation of the intensity of the factionalism. Finally, we understood that the ultimate responsiblity for aboriginal language maintenance lies with the speech communities themselves and success in keeping the language alive is a factor of their degree of ethnovitality. A school system may serve as an agency to institutionalize formal language programs to aid the process of linguistic and cultural maintenance. A school program is necessary but not sufficient in itself to maintain a language and culture. The responsibility rests with the speakers.

References

Barman, J., Hébert, Y. M., and McCaskill, D. (Eds.). *Indian Education in Canada: Vol. 1: The Legacy, and Vol. 2: Contemporary Perspectives.* Vancouver: University of British Columbia Press, 1986.

Bauman, R. and Sherzer, J. (Eds.). *Explorations in the Ethnography of Speaking.* New York: Cambridge University Press, 1974.

Dorr-Bremme, D. W. "Ethnographic Evaluation: A Theory and Method." *Educational Evaluation and Policy Analysis*, 1985, 7 (1), 65–83.

Driver, H. E. *Indians of North America.* 2nd ed. Chicago: University of Chicago Press, 1969.

Giles, H., Bourhis, R. Y., and Taylor, D. M. "Toward a Theory of Language in Ethnic Group Relations." In H. Giles (Ed.), *Language, Ethnicity, and Inter-Group Relations.* New York: Academic Press, 1977.

Guba, E. G., and Lincoln, Y. S. *Effective Evaluation: Improving the Usefulness of Evaluation Results Through Responsive and Naturalistic Approaches.* San Francisco: Jossey-Bass, 1981.

Hamers, J. and Blanc, M. *Bilingualité et bilinguisme* [Bilinguality and Bilingualism]. Bruxelles: Pierre Mardaga éditeur, 1983.

Hébert, Y. M. "The Sociopolitical Context of Native Indian Language Education in British Columbia." *Canadian Journal of Native Studies*, 1984, *4* (1), 121–137.

House, E. R. *Evaluating with Validity.* Beverly Hills, Calif.: Sage, 1980.

Hymes, D. *Foundations of Sociolinguistics: An Ethnographic Approach.* Philadelphia: University of Pennsylvania Press, 1974.

"Indian Self-Government in Canada." Report of the Special Committee of the House of Commons, Issue no. 4. Ottawa: Queen's Printer for Canada, 1984.

Longboat, D. "First Nations Control of Indian Education: The Path of Our Survival as Nations." In J. Barman, Y. M. Hébert, and D. McCaskill (Eds.), *Indian Education in Canada, Vol. 2: Contemporary Perspectives.* Vancouver: University of British Columbia Press, 1986.

National Indian Brotherhood. "Indian Control of Indian Education." Policy paper presented to the Minister of Indian Affairs and Northern Development. Ottawa, 1972.

Philips, S. U. "Some Sources of Cultural Variability in the Regulation of Talk." *Language in Society*, 1976, *5*, 81–95.

Philips, S. U. "Similarities in North American Indian Groups: Nonverbal Behavior and Their Relation to Early Child Development." Paper prepared for the Conference on Native American Interaction Patterns, University of Alberta, Edmonton, April 21–25, 1982.

Philips, S. U. *The Invisible Culture: Communication in Classroom and Community on the Warm Springs Indian Reservation.* New York: Longman, 1983.

Scollon, R., and Scollon, S. B. K. *Advances in Discourse Processes, Vol. 7: Narrative, Literacy and Face in Interethnic Communication.* New Jersey: Ablex, 1981.

Smolicz, J. J. *Culture and Education in a Plural Society.* Canberra, Australia: Curriculum Development Centre, 1979.

Stake, R. E. "Should Educational Evaluation Be More Objective or More Subjective? More Subjective!" Paper presented at annual meeting of American Educational Research Association, Toronto, April 1978.

Yvonne M. Hébert is assistant professor of French language education in the Department of Curriculum and Instruction at the University of Calgary, and was a Social Sciences and Humanities Research Council of Canada post-doctoral fellow in the faculty of Education, University of British Columbia, 1982–1984, and a Killam pre-doctoral fellow in theoretical linguistics and Indian languages, also at the University of British Columbia, 1977–1980.

Methodological design and implementation are often entangled in a web of ethical considerations.

Conceptual Crossroads: Methods and Ethics in Ethnographic Evaluation

David M. Fetterman

Naturalistic evaluation is not a monolithic entity. It is a generic term for many kinds of qualitative appraisals. Naturalistic inquiry (Lincoln and Guba, 1985), educational connoisseurship and criticism (Eisner, 1977), a "qualitative evaluation methods" approach (Patton, 1980), and ethnographic educational evaluation (Fetterman, 1984a; Fetterman and Pitman, 1986) are all forms of qualitative and naturalistic evaluation. The tools and designs used in these approaches are very similar. They all require ethical and methodological introspection. Each approach, however, has its own set of standards. The appropriate criteria should be used to judge the success or failure of each approach. One of the most prominent forms of naturalistic evaluation is ethnographic educational evaluation (Fetterman, 1986).

Ethnography is a personal science. The goal is to understand and describe people's perceptions of reality. Exploring the cognitive and affective domain of human beings requires sensitivity and training. The delicacy required of ethnographic work is nowhere more evident and more necessary than at the conceptual crossroads where methods and ethical decision making intersect. The ethnographer arrives at this crossroad when, in the pursuit of fieldwork, he or she must make intelligent and

D. D. Williams (Ed.). *Naturalistic Evaluation.*
New Directions for Program Evaluation, no. 30. San Francisco: Jossey-Bass, June 1986.

informed decisions that satisfy the demands of science and morality. This chapter addresses those moments of decision and attempts to put them in perspective by locating them within the lifecycle of ethnographic evaluation.

The ethnographic evaluator's development is often closely tied to the cyclical process of contract research; a pattern that characterizes the inception and growth not only of a particular project but of the evaluator's career as well. Each milestone requires its own moments of decision, when the ethnographer must accommodate both methodological needs and ethical obligations. In tying these milestones to some of my own moments of decision, I hope not only to mitigate these difficult times for other contract evaluators but also to clarify the nature of a decision-making process that continues throughout the ethnographer's professional life.

Lifecycle of the Ethnographer's Career

The lifecycle of both evaluator and project begins with the research proposal. Writing a proposal for funding lays the foundation and sets the tone of the study. Experienced ethnographic evaluators have learned to take charge during this phase when the project is first conceived. This is the period for establishing the budget—to provide for fieldworkers, equipment and time to think, analyze the data, and write up the findings. In writing the proposal, the ethnographer faces an early conflict of interest. The demands of contract and sponsor may collide with those of ethnographic work. The proposal will reflect either a creative solution or the evaluator's adaptation to the dominant (logical positivist) paradigm in evaluation research.

Evaluators must present their methodological intent in a clear and honest manner. Dishonesty, including significant omissions, will surface later in the project. Promising a qualitative product and not being able to deliver it will have a high cost for the evaluator, the research corporation, and the field. In one case in which I was called in to review a contractor's "qualitative" work, we found gross ignorance rather than gross negligence, malfeasance, or fraud. The evaluators had promised to conduct a qualitative study; however, they were only slightly familiar with some of the techniques and had no idea how to analyze the data or report the findings. Their five-hundred-page report was a meaningless, uninterpretable hodge-podge of pieces of information. This lackadaisical attitude toward evaluation was unethical. It cost the program a fair hearing before legislative analysts. It damaged the sponsor's credibility in selecting a reputable team of evaluators, and ultimately it cost some of the (nonseniority) evaluators their jobs. This does not even touch the damage done to the perception of the field by those effected by this academic sham.

Following the receipt of a contract, it is necessary to receive routine "check ups." Meetings are scheduled with the sponsor to reaffirm the promises and agreements made in the proposal. Evaluators have contractual obligations to fulfill their promises to their sponsor. Alternative strategies and topics can emerge during the study, however alterations must be mediated with the sponsor. Sponsors are usually reasonable and conscientious individuals and will accept a reasoned argument regarding significant methodological alterations (within the confines of what they have already promised their superiors). There are cases, however, in which different world views clash and no compromise is possible. In these cases, evaluators have an ethical obligation to stand by their original design, alter the design of the evaluation research only if appropriate, or withdraw from the contract.

Most ethical, methodological, and contractual surprises are mitigated if caught early. Periodically, however, gross misunderstandings can occur between contractors and their sponsors even in the early stages. In one case, I won a contract that was explicitly ethnographic in design. One week after the award, the sponsors demanded a change to a closed-questionnaire approach, with both the questions and the choice of interview subjects coming under their control. They also wanted us to provide compliance information about each of the programs and to increase the number of sites visited without altering the funding. As an ethnographic evaluator and project director, I found it necessary to take a firm stand against this mutilation of methodology, ethics, and fiscal administration. In this instance, we were able to convince the sponsors of the untenable ethical and fiscal problems some of their alterations imposed but were unable to come to a satisfactory solution to the radical methodological alterations imposed on the study. The sponsor's flip-flop in orientation appears, in retrospect, to have been in part a power play to establish their control over the study. The ethical issue that remained in this conflict required loyalty to the integrity of the methodology proposed and accepted. This case has entered litigation and is being argued on methodological-contractual grounds.

Childhood. Assuming a healthy beginning, the ethnographer's career enters its formative years. This period involves developing the ability to identify key actors and informants and make detailed schedules, appointments, and other plans to arrange for entrance into the field. During this period first impressions dominate interactions. Honesty is the only commodity ethnographic evaluators have to exchange for the trust of their informants. It is a fragile bond that is easily broken with the slightest, even inadvertent, transgression. The loss of trust may result from outright falsehood to simple ignorance of protocol.

Violating protocol is one of the more common errors that causes irreparable damage to a working relationship. It is critical, for example, for the ethnographic evaluator to recognize and respect the protocol of the site. Educational settings, for example, are governed by hierarchical relations. Permission from the superintendent must be granted before permission from a principal is proposed. The impact of protocol regarding one's ability to gain access to documents and people should not be underestimated. Respecting protocol can create a halo effect, and ignoring protocol can place obstacles in the ethnographer's path throughout the entire study.

During this phase of the ethnographer's career, extreme ethical dexterity may be required. The ethical obligations to maintain an implicit trust with and a nonjudgmental orientation toward informants may require toleration of bigotry, cruelty, and other reprehensible traits of the informant. In one instance, I was interviewing a powerful black leader regarding how he orchestrated political support for his program. During the middle of an informal late-night interview at his home, he explained to me why he would never hire a white person in his organization. He felt the issue of qualifications was not pertinent. He argued that hiring a white would be robbing a black of a job. Moreover, whites had made his life miserable, and hiring a white would be a form of "self-contempt and self-hatred."

This type of reverse discrimination from an individual whom one might expect to be intolerant of discrimination did not become an issue for the ethnographer at that time. The purpose of the meeting was to gain access to the leader's organization and to understand his world view. He was providing both of these to me in an extremely hospitable manner—in his own home. The reverse discrimination discussion was not forgotten. This data was used later in the study and as a guide to understanding the organizational dynamics of his institution. Individual names were never used or needed. Tolerance was required because the ethnographer had implicitly promised a trust and a nonjudgmental orientation.

Personal tolerance was stretched to its limits once when I was working as an assistant director and ethnographer in a senior citizen center. I was collecting initial interview data as a means of gaining the trust of program participants when I ran into Betsy. Betsy was a ninety-year-old woman and one of the sweetest and friendliest individuals I had ever met. During my first lengthy conversation with her, she began rambling on, half in German and half in English. I tried a few poorly asked questions in German about her youth and she began to open up. During the conversation I heard her repeat "Arbeit macht frei" over and over again. In time, I realized she was referring to the concentration camps. My first impression was that she was a survivor, much like the survivors I had worked with in Israel. Unfortunately, it did not take long to realize she was not a victim but a supporter of the Nazi movement. When I asked about the Jews and the Poles, she explained to me how "they deserved it," since they were the cause of the financial and moral bankruptcy of her country. She had organized rallies for the Nazis and remembered her one glorious moment when Adolf Hitler actually shook her hand. This was my link to the women in the center. Everyone loved her and she had befriended me. I had already extended an implicit trust. This was one of the most difficult ethical balancing acts I have had to entertain during this phase of ethnographic evaluation.

Ethnographers may also learn to develop a thick skin in some situations. In one mild example, I was "hanging-out" with some of my black inner city informants after school and spent a few hours listening to them talk about the local gangs and about this whitey and that whitey. Periodically, they would remind me that "I was an exception." It obviously was not the time to inform them that they were perpetuating the same type of racist behavior they abhorred. The objective was to learn what their concerns were and how they organized and interpreted their world.

Adolescence. Conducting fieldwork is much like re-entering adolescence. The field worker must learn a new language, new rituals, and a wealth of new cultural information. This period is marked by tremendous excitement, frustration, and confusion. The ethnographic evaluator exposes himself or herself to personal and professional turmoil as a part of the experience.

One of my first site visits for a research corporation that had never even heard of an ethnographer prior to my hiring is highly illustrative. I had convinced the researchers of the utility of the approach and was therefore under considerable pressure to show them a few interesting insights using ethnographic evaluation. I collected a mountain of material during the first two weeks, from interviews, observation, and documents. I sketched a few informal networks, and felt that I had accomplished a lot during a very short time.

On what was to have been the last day of the site visit a student befriended me. After a few hours of conversation about his life and the neighborhood, he decided to show me around. He introduced me to a number of the leaders running life in the streets. It was getting hot and he knew I was from California, so he brought me to a health food store for a cold drink and a snack. We went in and my new friend winked at the owner of the store and told him to give me a granola bar with some natural soda. I said thanks and reached out my hand for the granola bar and felt something else under the bar. It was a nickel bag of marijuana. I looked at the owner, then I looked at my friend. I did not want to show any form of disapproval or ingratitude, but this was not exactly what I had had in mind when I agreed to play the role of guest, visitor, and friend.

A moment later, I heard steps in perfect stride. I looked over to the front window and saw two policemen walking by, looking right in the window. My hand was still in the air with the mixed contents for all to see. My heart dropped to the floor. My first thought was, "I'm going to get busted. How am I going to explain this to my colleagues at the research corporation?"

Fortunately, the police disappeared as quickly as they had appeared. I asked my friend what had just transpired. He explained to me that the police were paid off regularly and would bother you only if they needed money or if an owner had not made a contribution. (This environment is similar to the environment of the racketeer described in Whyte's classic *Street Corner Society*, 1943, and Hippler's 1973 depiction of the inner city of Hunter's Point.)

After recovering emotionally and finishing the tour of the neighborhood, I went back to my hotel room and furiously wrote up the event. I later used it in one of my governmental reports to describe the neighborhood context of these students. This provided a context for assessing the relative success of an educational program that had tremendous competition for the students' attention. The incident was also useful in showing me that my informant was both proud of his cultural knowlege (knowing where to "cop dope") and yet capable of experimenting with a conventional lifestyle by entering the educational program under study. This experience reveals some of the benefits of living and working in a natural setting, as well as the role of serendipity in fieldwork (see Fetterman, 1984b).

During this adolescent period the ethnographic evaluator begins to gather the strands of information that will form the fabric of his or her understanding of the culture. The ethnographic evaluator's ability to gather this information relies on an early recognition of the formal and informal power brokers within a community and a school. Establishing contacts with the clergy, politicians, local business people, police, and gang leaders opened doors for me throughout my national study of dropouts, potential dropouts, and "push outs." Identifying with one group or the other will shut down important lines of communication and allow the ethnographic evaluator access to only half the story. On an administrative level this role is generally understood; however, sometimes things go wrong.

During one study, I was standing near the reception room of the school office when the secretary asked me to meet her after school to discuss a former employee. I agreed to the meeting, recognizing that the school office was not an environment conducive to open discussion. When I met her, I found that she had arranged a secret meeting between me and the former employee. I listened to the former employee, who explained why she had been fired by the new director. She provided me with a picture of a dictatorial atmosphere in which teachers feared for their jobs every day of their lives. At first, I took this information with a grain of salt, as she was obviously bitter. But after a reasonable amount of digging and luck I found her assessment honest and accurate.

A few months later, at a dinner meeting in Detroit, the director of the program informed me that he did not like me going behind his back to speak to former staff members and that he had contemplated taking out an underworld contract on me for "stabbing him in the back" in that fashion. No information had been reported, but he wanted all communication to be cleared through him.

I explained to him that I was sorry he felt that way but that I felt an obligation to speak to the former employee, particularly since I had known her while she had still been on the staff. In addition, I had no warning that I would be meeting her. Third, I explained to him that if the situation came up, I would do the same thing again. I had a professional obligation as an ethnographer and an evaluator to listen to all parties interested in contacting me.

The director and I were able to reconcile our differences during that evening in Detroit. I am reasonably certain, however, that he never understood why I was compelled to behave in a manner he construed as illicit. Moreover, this required behavior pattern on my part cost me much useful information from him during the period in which he misunderstood my actions. This is just one of the potentially life-threatening reactions that can result from "studying up" the social structure. (See Nader, 1969, and Harrell-Bond, 1976, for a more detailed discussion of studying the elite in society.)

Generally, a constructive orientation can be conveyed to administration by playing the role of a management consultant—informing management of positive and negative elements of their system, with the aim of improving the system's operation. On a student level, all that is necessary is to be honest about the two halves of one's role—part student trying to understand how the system works and part professional evaluator trying to come up with recommendations to improve the school program.

Adolescent students possess a psychological "radar" that tells them if someone is being honest. If they sense any dishonesty or insincerity, they can undermine the value of any study. In addition, they justifiably come to expect a reasonable measure of reciprocity. As a teacher-researcher in an inner city school, I remember receiving a phone call late one night from one of my students who was also a key informant. His call came from jail. He had been charged with carrying a concealed weapon and needed assistance. I helped him secure legal defense and maintain his position in school. The other teachers frowned on this type of behavior, but I explained that as a teacher and as a human being I had an obligation to my students both inside and outside the classroom. In addition, as an ethnographer I tried to explain to them the ethical obligation of maintaining reciprocity with informants. My superiors did not understand or appreciate this behavior, which they felt was out of character for a professional educator, but for an ethnographic evaluator this professional obligation was met by reflex.

One of the dangers of this period is miscalculating the appropriate degree of reciprocity required. Ethnographic evaluators can be targets for informants who feed them the information they think the ethnographic evaluator wants to hear in order to collect the reward for that information.

Another problem that can emerge is fieldwork paralysis. Ethnographic evaluators, like conventional ethnographers, attempt to remain as unobtrusive as possible. Unfortunately, this can be carried to an extreme. I have observed cases in which my own staff felt unable to collect any information for fear of disrupting the system. They overdramatized the sensitivities of their prospective informants and withdrew from any data collection. After I convinced one of them to break the ice with a few non-threatening questions, he realized that he had projected his own concerns on the informant and that the system was not quite as delicate as he had assumed. In a second case, the staff member had to be replaced.

A similar danger can occur in the field when a fieldworker goes native. In one case, a staff member felt so strongly affiliated with the group under study that he decided to join them and leave his data-collection responsibilities behind. Ethnography is a personal science, and individuals must make personal decisions about how they are going to live their lives, even in the middle of a study. Careful consideration, however, should go into the decision to enter any role that may have competing obligations and responsibilities. The cost to the study and to the sponsors, and to the credibility of co-workers, can be devastating. An ethnographic evaluator should err on the side of professionalism and responsibility; a large number of people rely on the data evaluators provide, ranging from the sponsors to the students in the programs being evaluated.

Adulthood. The ethnographic evaluator reaches maturity when he or she has gained acceptance into the community or school under study. Acceptance improves the quality of data by opening up new levels of previously undisclosed symbols and cultural knowledge. The question of disclosing sacred cultural knowledge becomes more problematic after the ethnographic evaluator reaches this adult stage of the lifecycle.

In an extremely sensitive situation, it was necessary to withhold potentially explosive information. One afternoon, while interviewing one of the students in an experimental program, I heard a scream. I left the student and ran up the flight of stairs to the source. The principal was already twenty feet ahead of me. He was pounding on the door, trying to force it open. The sounds emanating from the room were by then more pronounced and sensual in tone. The principal forced the door open. I was standing directly behind him. We found one of the guidance counselors sexually engaged with a student in the program. They had been upright against the door and were now half upright and half on the floor. The counselor was discreetly dismissed and the student was temporarily dismissed and referred to an appropriate and responsible counseling center.

The principal and I spent the evening discussing the problem and what our mutual responsibilities were in the incident. I was convinced that this was an atypical situation and that the principal had handled the matter appropriately. We knew that reporting this incident to the sponsors would permanantly close the school down. As an ethnographic evaluator, I was faced with a myriad of individuals to whom I had ethical obligations ranging from the taxpayer to the students in the program. I decided not to report the incident for the good of the program, the more conscientious staff members, and the students who were benefitting from the program. Aside from the implicit trust shared with the informants, this decision was conceptually guided by a traditional risk or cost-benefit analysis (Reynolds, 1979). In addition, reporting the incident would have represented a form of methodological suicide.

On another level, adulthood for the ethnographic evaluator is knowing when you are wearing your ethnographer's cap and when you are wearing your evaluator's cap. This may sound simplistic, but in fact it is not time-bound or purely situationally directed. An ethnographic evaluator is always collecting information throughout the study, whether in the streets or in plush conference rooms in Washington. Similarly, the ethnographic evaluator continually appraises how well the system works, whether it is the system of administering funding for the program or the system of classroom instruction. The key to being a mature ethnographic evaluator is, first, knowing when to allow one approach to dominate one's mode of operation and second, knowing how to present oneself before the right audiences.

There is a delicate balance between collecting enough information and making an assessment. Additional information will always be informative. There is, however, a law of diminishing returns in any endeavor. There are also many time pressures—sponsor deadlines and proposal writing for the next project, to name a few. Judgments must be made to allow the next stage of the study to begin. The ethnographic evaluator must constantly guard against making assessments prematurely. At the same time he or she must be able to get at the heart of an issue and often make best guesses about the fate of a school.

I encountered a difficult decision of this nature several years ago involving the fate of one of the educational programs for dropouts (discussed earlier). Based on a site visit and other available information, the sponsors were unhappy with the progress of a particular program and did not want to wait for the results of the study, which was only one-third complete at the time. They informed us that they were ready to make a negative decision regarding the continued funding of the program. They asked for our assessment of the program before all the data had been collected, analyzed, and synthesized. We objected to being put in this position and informed them that we would not be a part of such a travesty.

The phone call ended with this ultimatum: Either we provide insights into the program or, if we maintained our ethical stance, they would act on the information they did (or did not) have in hand. They gave us two-and-a-half hours to think about it before calling us back.

We sat there stunned, irritated, and unsure. We went over the reasons for not disclosing any information about the program. Then a few pragmatic arguments were made for providing our opinions to the sponsors. Reluctantly, we decided that some input would be better than no input, given the circumstances. Unfortunately, we did not have much data to go on. The traditional evaluators had only some of the pretests. The scores were terrible, which was expected because they were scores received prior to treatment in the program. I went through my precoded, preanalyzed field notes and found a few points that could be interpreted in favor of the program and a few against. In sum, we pooled our information and took our best guess. We believed that the program merited further funding and further consideration.

The ethnographic data were useful on two levels. First, they documented when the sponsors had collected their information and what kind of information they had collected. Thus, I was able to explain that the reason they had not seen any students during their visit was because it had been during the middle of the summer and it had been at four thirty (after regular school hours). Second, the attendance data they had examined did look bad but depended on one's perspective. The average attendance level was less than 60 percent. The sponsors were comparing this program's attendance figure with local school attendance reports of 70 to 75 percent average daily attendance. The students in this program were not to be compared to the average student in the regular school, however. These were students who had dropped out of the neighborhood schools—they were the regular non-attendees. I added a sense of proportion and context to the discussion by explaining that in this case the local school baseline was not appropriate. The accurate baseline to use was zero percent attendance because these students were dropouts. This made 55 percent attendance look surprisingly good.

These arguments, in conjunction with additional anecdotes, ended up saving the program. In a more pristine ethnographic endeavor, it is unlikely that these pressures would have surfaced. External pressures are a routine part of applied anthropology—particularly ethnographic educational evaluation. In this case, it was crucial that the ethnographic data be used as appropriately as possible, but the information had to be presented in the form of an evaluator's appraisal of program progress. (See Pierce-Colfer, 1976, for another case study illustrating similar ethical dilemmas.)

On a more superficial level, literally knowing when to wear an ethnographer's cap and when to wear an evaluator's cap is the sign of adulthood. Apparel can be symbolically significant to many colleagues in evaluation. For example, an unwritten dress code may require a tie. This is a small price to pay for establishing an initial level of credibility as a professional. Most anthropologists would wear a loin cloth if they thought it was appropriate in another culture but may give little thought to fitting into a subculture closer to home. At the very least, an ethnographic evaluator should be sensitive to the norms of his or her group and not attempt to make a judgmental statement about the cultural practice. An ethnographic evaluator should have enough experience with the educational and evaluation subcultures to know how to act or how to get around conforming in an appropriate (nondisruptive and nonobtrusive) manner. This example may appear petty, but it is a manifestation of a mind set that may have larger implications as a study unfolds.

Similarly, at advisory panel meetings or professional association meetings or in the classroom, it is important to know when to argue as an evaluator and when it is imperative to be a participant-observer. In advisory panel meetings, a ritual common to evaluations in which experts sit in judgment of the progress of the study, an ethnographic evaluator must be prepared to be a player in the politics of emergent vested interests. This role requires an adept evaluator or politician to maintain the integrity of the study, defend its progress, and mold it in the right direction. During the same meeting, as ethnographer, he or she presents descriptions, patterns, and preliminary findings for discussion. It is incumbent on the ethnographic evaluator to become a cognitive code switcher. This requires him or her to think in two conceptual frameworks simultaneously—addressing concerns of reliability and validity (from a logical positivist's perspective), and at the same time ensuring a phenomenologically based study.

Family. The ethnographic evaluator's family includes not only the interdisciplinary team but the network of colleagues in the field as well. Colleagues serve as a quality control to maintain methodological rigor. Often innovations are required when working as an ethnographic evaluator, and working at the cutting edge of research is an exhilarating but unsettling experience. There is no place with a greater need for judiciously imposed quality controls. Effective ethnographic evaluators use members of the team to test their ideas. They solicit opinions from scholars from different disciplines to determine if a specific adaptation will address methodological concerns across disciplines. This is particularly important when attempting to combine ethnographic, survey, and experimental or quasi-experimental designs in the same evaluation study. Similarly, a network of ethnographic evaluation colleagues can be used to test the appropriateness of such novel methodological innovations as, for example, projective techniques and short-term multi-site fieldwork schedules.

This network is established and maintained by telephone, correspondence, professional meetings, scholarly literature, and computer communications. The Bitnet (Because It's Time computer network), EARN (European Academic Research Network), and ARPANET (Advanced Research Projects Agency) systems facilitate communication. These systems link over fourteen hundred computer nodes together, connecting universities and research centers throughout the world, ranging from the City University of New York to Stanford University and from the Universidad de Barcelona in Spain to Haifa University in Israel. Brief messages, letters, and manuscripts are shared through an electronic mail system. This type of network provides feedback that can be measured in nanoseconds (Fetterman, 1985).

This network, like any system, is dependent on the integrity of the people that function within it. Ethnographic evaluators share preliminary findings in search of an honest critique of their work. An uncritical review reduces the quality of the work produced and the reputation of the field. Uncritical reviews can result from reasons ranging from expedience to misguided friendship. Critiques can be both critical and diplomatic. The most significant abuse of this network is theft. The theft of ideas in any field of endeavor undermines the efforts required to build a network in which a free exchange of ideas and information is encouraged.

In one study, a formerly prominant member of the field used my work in an unauthorized and unacknowledged manner. Specifically, he reproduced a great deal of my work—word for word. In fact, he did it twice. When the matter was brought to his attention, he refused to provide a reason for the unacceptable behavior the first time it occurred. The second time was dismissed in a cursory fashion as an omission. After providing the individual with numerous opportunities to provide a satisfactory response and receiving only threats to my career, it was necessary to bring the case to the academy in print. The behavior could not be condoned as it tarnishes the credibility and integrity of all scientists and does irreparable damage to the trust required to maintain an atmosphere of free intellectual exchange, not to mention the methodological ramifications that result from such an abuse (Fetterman, 1981).

Retiring. The ethnographic evaluator lives a relatively fast-paced life while working on a project. When projects end, the ethnographic evaluator must be able to wrap up his or her work and move on. Ethnographic evaluators immerse themselves in the field, like conventional ethnographers. This long-term personal involvement can make it difficult to recognize when participant-observation has ended. The ethnographic evaluator has a responsibility to his or her team, the network of coresearchers, to disengage from his or her segment of the study at the appropriate time. This often involves beginning the disengagement process before all the findings have been reported and the money spent. (See Rose's 1964 theory of disengagement for retired individuals for comparison.)

The ethnographic evaluator's talents may be needed elsewhere. New proposals need to be written if continuity and quality are to be maintained. In addition, coresearchers often need the ethnographic information to help them interpret their own segments of the study. They cannot wait for a self-indulgent enthnographer to dawdle with the delivery of his or her findings.

Last Rites. There is a final stage for some ethnographic educational evaluators and that is recognizing when to leave the discipline entirely. Methodological sloppiness, job burnout, and a significant shift in disciplinary interests mark the point at which it is time to shift gears and leave ethnographic pursuits to the next generation. A lack of commitment to this enterprise has devastating effects on the quality of the profession and, in turn, on how it is perceived by the outside world. In addition, ethnographic educational evaluation is a highly demanding profession personally. Conducting ethnographic evaluations places the ethnographic evaluator in a schedule in which he or she is away from home for months. The insecurity of federal funding, the pressures of proposal competition to support staff members, arguments with sponsors regarding deadlines and methodological designs, and arguments with colleagues in the process of creating a new field can take their toll. Not knowing when to completely disengage can be lethal—mentally and physically.

Conclusion

Methods and ethics are inseparable in ethnographic evaluation. Methodological design and implementation require ethical reflection. The simplest methodological approach can present the ethnographer with convoluted, tormenting decisions. The ethical overtones associated with any number of specific data-gathering techniques can be overwhelming. The ethnographer must use his or her judgment continually throughout the field experience to prevent incidents that cause harm to individuals or to science. An insensitive approach toward matters with significant ethical ramifications can result in a sabotaged research design or data-collection strategy. Similarly, a lack of tact or concern with the manner in which findings are reported can cause irreparable harm to those under study and can justifiably close all doors for future research of any kind in that area.

The ethnographer must balance ethical obligations with the need to collect the data required to answer fundamental questions. He or she must learn enough to explain how people perceive the world without climbing into a shell for fear of disturbing anyone's sensitivities. Examining the conceptual crossroads of methods and ethics in ethnographic evaluation through the lifecycle of an ethnographer's career portrays a dimension of ethnographic work rarely revealed. I hope this view of the subtle intricacies of the profession will be reflexive in raising questions about the personal nature of educational research in general.

36

References

Eisner, E. W. "On the Uses of Educational Connoisseurship and Criticism for Evaluating Classroom Life." *Teachers College Record,* 1977, *78* (3), 345-358.

Fetterman, D. M. "New Perils for the Contract Ethnographer." *Anthropology and Education Quarterly,* 1981, *12* (1), 71-80.

Fetterman, D. M. (Ed.) *Ethnography in Educational Evaluation.* Beverly Hills, Calif.: Sage, 1984a.

Fetterman, D. M. "Guilty Knowledge, Dirty Hands, and Other Ethical Dilemmas: The Hazards of Contract Research." In D. M. Fetterman (Ed.), *Ethnography in Educational Evaluation.* Beverly Hills, Calif.: Sage, 1984b.

Fetterman, D. M. "The CAE Network." *Anthropology Newsletter,* 1985, *26* (1), 8.

Fetterman, D. M. "Ethnographic Educational Evaluation." In G. D. Spindler (Ed.), *Educational Anthropology Now.* New York: Academic Press, 1986.

Fetterman, D. M., and Pitman, M. A. (Eds.). *Ethnographic Evaluation: Theory, Practice, and Politics.* Beverly Hills, Calif.: Sage, 1986.

Harrell-Bond, B. "Studying Elites: Some Special Problems." In M. A. Rynkiewich and J. P. Spradley (Eds.), *Ethics and Anthropology: Dilemmas in Fieldwork.* New York: Wiley, 1976.

Hippler, A. E. "The Game of Black and White at Hunters Point." In T. Weaver (Ed.), *To See Ourselves: Anthropology and Modern Social Issues.* Glenview, Ill.: Scott, Foresman, 1973.

Lincoln, Y. S. and Guba, E. G. *Naturalistic Inquiry.* Beverly Hills, Calif.: Sage, 1985.

Nader, L. "Up the Anthropologist—Perspectives Gained from Studying Up." In D. Hymes (Ed.), *Reinventing Anthropology.* New York: Random House, 1969.

Patton, M. Q. *Qualitative Evaluation Methods.* Beverly Hills, Calif.: Sage, 1980.

Pierce-Colfer, C. J. "Rights, Responsibilities, and Reports: An Ethical Dilemma in Contract Research." In M. A. Rynkiewich and J. P. Spradley (Eds.), *Ethics and Anthropology: Dilemmas in Fieldwork.* New York: Wiley, 1976.

Reynolds, P. D. *Ethical Dilemmas and Social Science Research.* San Francisco: Jossey-Bass, 1979.

Rose, A. M. "A Current Theoretical Issue in Social Gerontology." *Gerontologist,* 1964, *4,* 46-50.

Whyte, W. F. *Street Corner Society: The Social Structure of an Italian Slum.* Chicago: University of Chicago, 1943.

David M. Fetterman is a senior member of Stanford University administration. Concurrently, he is an assistant professor in the School of Education at Stanford University. Fetterman has received awards from the Evaluation Research Society and the Washington Association for Professional Anthropologists for his ethnographic contributions to evaluation.

There are circumstances in which the evaluator can
and should choose to use multiple methods and
approaches to answer evaluative questions.

The Whole Is Greater: Combining Qualitative and Quantitative Approaches in Evaluation Studies

Mary Lee Smith

It happened during a postmortem of a recent evaluation of the practices and effects of retaining children for a second year in kindergarten. I (the qualitative or naturalistic analyst) complained that no one remembered anything about the study except its statistical outcomes. My colleague, Lorrie Shepard (the quantitative analyst) confessed jealousy of my direct contact with the rich and meaningful evidence from interviews with teachers and observations of classrooms. I was "close" to the data; she was quoted in the headlines of the newspaper. But neither of us could imagine the separate parts of the study standing alone and making the impact it did.

This chapter is the outcome of a belief that, in evaluation, the whole is greater than the sum of the parts when qualitative and quantitative approaches and methods are combined. Some circumstances in which both approaches can be effectively combined are considered. Finally, I will present the case histories of two evaluation studies in which Shepard and I collaborated in the use of multiple methods. Although most methodological papers in evaluation are deductive and theoretical, focusing on

D. D. Williams (Ed.). *Naturalistic Evaluation.*
New Directions for Program Evaluation, no. 30. San Francisco: Jossey-Bass, June 1986.

definitions and distinctions, I choose to study methods the same way I study schools or other social institutions, by examining cases and examples, deriving some tentative propositions, and seeing what conclusions can be drawn.

A brief digression from this purpose is made necessary by the difference in terminology in the title of this chapter, which uses the word *qualitative,* and the title of this issue of *New Directions in Program Evaluation,* which uses the term *naturalistic.* For the purposes of this chapter, a qualitative approach involves the long-term and first-hand study of a case by the investigator for the purpose of understanding and describing human action in the context of that case. Field methods are used to collect data, including direct observation of action in its natural context, clinical interviews to elicit the multiple meanings of participants in that case, and collection of documents. A qualitative approach leads to reports primarily in the form of words, pictures, and displays rather than formal models or statistical findings.

In my view, *qualitative* is a broader term than *naturalistic* or *ethnographic* and encompasses both inductive and hypothetico-deductive processes of inquiry as well as disciplines not limited to anthropology. When referring to the work and terminology of others, the best tactic seems to be to describe and classify studies according to the following dimensions: long- versus longer-term data collection, focused versus not focused on cultural constructs, primarily inductive versus deductive, prespecified versus flexible designs, descriptive versus explanatory.

Two further assumptions of this chapter must be identified. First, the argument for the validity of qualitative approaches in evaluation has already been made (see Guba and Lincoln, 1981; Patton, 1980). Second, the animosity between advocates of qualitative and quantitative approaches has diminished, and the prevailing view is more conciliatory. Reichardt and Cook (1979) conclude that the antagonism between paradigms, between the philosophies of realism and idealism, was not inextricably linked with a conflict over choice of research methods. Their argument is persuasive and need not be repeated here.

Circumstances in Which Qualitative and Quantitative Approaches May Be Fruitfully Combined

When the Object of Evaluation Must Be Described. Good description is a commonly accepted standard for any evaluation. The policy, program, or product should be described well enough so that judgments of its worth can be made. Even advocates of the most rigorous, experimental evaluation models acknowledge that the program to be evaluated must be implemented for its effects to be observed. Its implementation must be documented. The imputation of causality of effects to the treatment rests on this documentation. Documentary evidence about the failure of the treatment to be delivered as intended may provide one explanation for negative or negligible effects in an experiment. How then, would documentation be accomplished? There is often no substitute for the narrative account produced by a sensitive observer. This person may be aided by a few rating scales on the important features of the treatment and whether they occurred, but the real value of such observation is the systematic, concrete, and accurate rendering of the details of the delivery of the treatment.

There is but a small step from the "thin description" of the events themselves to the "thick description" (Geertz, 1973) or to the examination of the meaning of events to the participants and understanding of the context in which they occurred. Sensitivity to context is essential for qualitative observers. *Context* itself is an overused but misunderstood term. When one considers the context of, say, a classroom, one must think of the physical space and objects within it, their arrangement, and the relationship between space, objects, and people, as well as density and climate. The relationships among people in the class establish a psychosocial context. The children bring to school a set of influences from their families, social classes, ethnic groups, and personal tendencies, all of which form the "ground" in a figure-ground Gestalt. The training and personal qualities of the teacher and the prior learning of the pupils are part of the educational context. Another part of context is the purpose for which individual events and the larger enterprise exist (for example, maintaining order and achieving instructional goals). The participants in the class hold different meanings for classroom events, and there is a collective "sense" of what is going on (McDermott and others, 1978).

Knowing the context makes symbolic activity interpretable. When the teacher flicks the light switch off and on, he or she has an intent (to quiet the children), and the act has a history involving the way the pattern and its meanings were established. Similarly, the principal's use of the intercom may interrupt classroom learning, establish routine, or connect the teacher with a hierarchical structure of authority, depending on the context. Even the foregoing oversimplification of context shows that a program is not introduced into a sterile laboratory but into a complex scheme of things, each of which has a bearing on the success of the program. Thus, to ignore the complexity of the background is to impoverish the evaluation. Britan (1981) asserts that ethnographic evaluation is contextual evaluation.

In addition to documenting context, qualitative descriptions of programs provide authenticity and may confirm or disconfirm assumptions that program developers have about the logical relations between program content and expected outcomes. In our study of the effects of the program Outward Bound (Smith and others, 1976), we were asked to provide "scientific evidence" that this wilderness experience affected those psychological characteristics identified in the goals of the program. We designed instruments to measure four such characteristics—self-assertion, self-esteem, self-awareness, and acceptance of others—and administered them in a time-series quasi-experiment. However, we asked that the evaluation include a participant observation study of the program to see whether there was any part of the experience that might plausibly change these characteristics in the participants. An excerpt from the report follows.

> The next day the entire patrol started on our first long alpine expedition. We hiked all day, coping as best we could with the different hiking speeds. Late in the afternoon we had not yet reached the projected camp site. By our own idiosyncratic process of decision making, we determined that the two strongest hikers would push ahead to locate the camp before sunset and guide the rest of us in. We hiked until it grew dark and once nearly missed the trail. Walking became laborious when the terrain unexpectedly turned to swamp. Our packs, recently loaded with food, settled into sore spots on shoulders and hips. We were plodding, making little progress, with no sign of our advance troop. Finally a light appeared in the distance, someone signaling us with a flashlight. We signaled back and kept sloshing. The night was cold, and we hadn't eaten. The Rio Grande, just wide enough to be troublesome, lay between us and the camp. The water was fast. It was too dark to see where to step, so the only method was to take off your boots and feel your way through the rocks. With a sense of resignation, I tied my boots to my pack and waded through the icy water. From behind me I heard Chris whimpering; she had lost her sneakers and couldn't make it. Not pausing to question myself, I dropped my pack on the bank, waded back and carried Chris on my back across the stream, then crossed for the third time to carry her pack. By that time my feet were so numb and my body so fatigued that I stumbled over a rock and fell [p. 417].
>
> Chris's life was beauty contests, formal dances, and "Daddy." She came to Outward Bound with purple nail polish and an expensive coiffure. On the first day she accosted the instructor, demanding that he help her with a recalcitrant sleeping bag zipper. During the first week she suffered stomach aches and homesickness. Everyone thought of her as a crier and complainer. In each new situation she whined that she couldn't do it and wouldn't do it; then she would stumble in and do it, complaining the entire time. I decided that Outward Bound was especially designed for people like Chris. She had never worked, never been challenged, never really lived. The course forced her into a series of compacted experiences, causing

her maturation to be accelerated. One could almost see her stamina and confidence grow as the course progressed. She tried hard but could not give up her ploy of professing weakness and hiding her strength. The stratagem must have worked for her; didn't it get her a free ride across the Rio Grande on my back [pp. 417–418]?

The evaluation team concluded that, contrary to the goals and expectations of the program managers that Outward Bound would build cohesiveness, cooperation, and acceptance of others, the actual experiences on the patrol (mutual dependency among patrol members and their differences in ability, fitness, and personality) might just as plausibly have had the opposite effect. The actual events that made up Outward Bound were fairly uniform, but the meanings held by participants about the events, and the ongoing interactions among the participants created a context that impinged on the effectiveness of the program.

When the Results of a Qualitative Study Can Be Extended. The antipathy between proponents of qualitative and quantitative paradigms has largely obscured the fact that even the purists among ethnographers regularly use questionnaires, structured observation schedules, and interview guides. Structured procedures of data collection are used to confirm or extend categories and propositions revealed in naturalistic studies. Suppose an evaluator observes the use of computers in a first-grade classroom to gauge the effectiveness of an in-service program in computer-assisted instruction. The evaluator interprets the data such that the real meaning of computer use in this classroom is to provide relief for a tired teacher. This is a category of use that was unanticipated in the original design yet important enough that the evaluator designs a test of its generality. A structured observation and interview study is arranged to test the proposition both in the original classroom and in other classrooms involved in the program. Sieber (1973) describes ways that surveys can augment the findings of qualitative research.

When Case Studies Can Be Targeted. One of the main criticisms of qualitative approaches is that selection of cases is not representative and that the findings are, therefore, of limited generalizability. Leaving aside the counterarguments that qualitative reports enhance naturalistic generalization (Stake, 1978), assume this criticism has merit. There are ways in which the selection of cases or persons and incidents within cases may be informed by results of surveys or existing research or theory, thus enhancing generalizability in the conventional sense. Results of preliminary surveys may establish that cases differ systematically according to such variables as geographic distribution, ethnicity, age, or sex composition of the population. Those cases that match significant combinations of these variables can then be chosen for intensive qualitative study. Pure induction may be sacrificed in this kind of design, for the evaluator must decide in advance what dimensions are important. When the observers get into the field, they may find that local circumstances are more influential than the dimensions originally used to select the cases. Nevertheless, the multisite, targeted case study is emerging as a popular design, especially in large-scale, federal projects (Firestone and Herriott, 1984; Smith and Robbins, 1984).

When Triangulation Will Improve Validity. An evaluator with a multioperation, multimethod paradigm will seek to design studies that fit that model. From Campbell (described by Collins, 1981) comes the idea that any one operationalization (for example, defining the construct "adjustment" as the score on the Smith Inventory of Adjustment) represents only a partial view of the construct. Every measure has an error of a certain kind, and any perspective from which a measure is taken (for example, self-report, report by other, report by observer) carries with it a degree of bias associated with that perspective. The sources of error and bias from alternative measures of the same phenomenon ought to be independent and cancel each other. What is left over, what is confirmed and corroborated by the various measures, represents the most valid picture of the phenomenon. In evaluation studies, experiments may control threats to internal validity of a causal claim. Yet experiments are nearly always contrived and unnatural and may frequently be threatened by "demand characteristics."

On the other hand, qualitative studies provide more natural and ecologically valid evidence, yet suffer perhaps from observer effects and identification of the researcher with the subjects through extensive personal contact. Questionnaires are reactive and oversimplify multiple meanings, but offer representative and easily standardized data. Each form of data collection has a strength as well as a weakness. In Campbell's framework (described by Collins, 1981), triangulation across many forms of measurement establishes that some phenomenon exists independently of a researcher's efforts to measure it. According to Collins (1981, p. 402), "Any measurement procedure is an imperfect pointer, constitutes a method-bound indicator, captures only a partial manifestation of the real-world entity, and contains much that is unique to the perspective used." The multi-method design "diversifies bias" and strives for "maximally divergent" assessment of program effects. Nothing could diversify bias more readily than a design that combines a hypothesis-testing experiment with observation and clinical interview conducted without a priori hypotheses. Only in a multimethod study could one ask whether the results of questionnaire surveys confirm the results of informant interviews or whether analysis of archival documents leads to different conclusions than the results of experiments. Attempts to triangulate findings of multimethod studies may either be planned in advance (implying a deductive sequence) or post hoc and fortuitous. Denzin (1971) details several types of triangulation, any of which may strengthen the interpretations and judgments that are the goal of evaluation.

When the Design of Multiple Studies Can Be Mutually Informative.
Qualitative and quantitative analysts may work as a team with information emerging from the qualitative observation and interviews fed to the quantitative researcher who designs instruments and samples occasions for systematic observation. The quantitative study is thus better informed about the ways the participants define terms and view the program and is better attuned to significant dimensions on the site. In turn the quantitative analyst feeds his or her partner preliminary data on what might be fruitful to examine in the field. Mutually informed studies do not meet the standards of multimethod triangulation, since they are not designed and executed independently and thus share error. However, this approach is advocated by Saxe and Fine (1979) as the best means of identifying "those program elements requiring revision or special attention" (p. 64).

When Attention Is Paid to Information Needs of Different Audiences.
Cronbach (1982) describes the trade-offs between the desiderata of fidelity (rigorous control over causal inferences) and bandwidth (representativeness) in designing evaluations. He argues that to address the political interests and information needs of stakeholders, the evaluator must spread resources so that evidence is obtained to allow these various groups to engage intelligently in policy formation. Some groups are likely to find results of quantitative (high-fidelity) approaches more persuasive. Others are likely to be influenced by qualitative reports. There is currently no adequate means of classifying audiences according to which form of report they believe or whose recommendations they accept. However, relevant to this discussion is Rein's (1976) suggestion that tacit knowledge, which has also been referred to as working knowledge, implicit beliefs, and world images, is more readily affected by stories and anecdotes than by statistical results, and in turn it affects an individual's generalizations and actions. House (1980) wrote that the evaluator's use of metaphors, dramatic structure, and other elements of story-telling has a direct effect on the reader's tacit beliefs.

No matter how much the personal beliefs of a formal authority in an institution are influenced by stories, he or she may feel obliged to base final decisions on the results of a rigorous experiment or survey. The managers of Outward Bound touted the results of the quasi-experiment, which demonstrated some positive effects, but belittled the qualitative report, calling it little better than the journal of a typical participant (among qualitative methodologists, this would have been more a compliment than a criticism). There was consternation among the project monitors of the Case Studies of Science Education (Stake and Easley, 1978) when the studies were referred to as just "cute little stories" (Brown, 1980). Yet in the synthesis (Harms and Yager, 1981) of the case studies, a representative survey and literature review, all of which were commissioned by the National Science Foundation to determine the status of science education, one can see that the experts relied most heavily on the findings of the case studies. Apparently, even the tacit knowledge of experts can be influenced by stories. Combining forms of evidence likely to influence both tacit and propositional knowledge covers all bases.

An Example: The Evaluation of
Learning Disabilities Identification

A local school district experienced difficulty with its formula for determining the eligibility of children for special education programs for the learning-disabled. Although administrators requested a psychometric study of cut-off scores, regression estimates, and counts of false-positives, I designed a naturalistic study of procedures used for identification. Among other things, the report demonstrated that the district's policy and statistical formula were not used at all by staff in the separate schools, who relied more on an idiosyncratic sense of which of the children needed academic help and "identified" them as learning disabled. Furthermore, an elaborate legalistic ritual had grown up to justify the school's identifications and to satisfy state and federal regulations. Diagnostic procedures were multifaceted but matched no known professional standards for valid measurement. The report failed to make an impact on district policies, perhaps because it was exclusively qualitative in form or perhaps because existing practices satisfied some entrenched institutional and professional interests (Smith, 1982). However, the report came to the attention of some Colorado legislators who were concerned about the dramatic increase in the learning-disabled population, and they commissioned a state-wide study of this issue (see Davis and Smith, 1984, for the political history of the study).

In designing the study, Shepard and I felt that the most persuasive study would be one with the strongest quantitative design but with a concrete and compelling narrative account as well. The quantitative portions of the study included an analysis of the costs of the process of identification, surveys of perceptions of the professional groups involved with identification, analysis of rates of prevalence of the learning disabled in Colorado, and a survey of pupils currently identified as learning disabled to document their characteristics. The qualitative portions of the evaluation included a linguistic analysis of definitions and diagnostic criteria of learning disabilities, a critique of tests used in identification, interviews with directors of special education, and a qualitative analysis of case records of pupils so identified.

The Quantitative Side. A multistage sampling design was used to ensure a representative sample of one thousand from the case files of pupils identified as learning disabled throughout the state. Eight hundred were subjected to a content analysis that included information on the pupils' intelligence and achievement scores (as well as many other traits), the personnel involved in decision making, the basis on which the decision was made, the treatment assigned as the result of placement, and the like.

Reliability and validity of coding procedures were established, and the sampling design suffered less than 5 percent "nonresponse."

The analysis was intended to answer the question: What are the characteristics of pupils identified as learning disabled? In its simple form, it involved a categorization of pupils and tabulation of the proportion of the sample within categories (for example, 23 percent of the sample had reliable evidence of a statistical discrepancy between IQ and achievement—a defining characteristic of learning disabilities). A more complex analysis sorted pupils into categories based on a combination of characteristics. For example, a pupil was placed in a category called "slow learner" if he or she had an IQ below 90 but no discrepancy between IQ and achievement, and no evidence of a perceptual-processing difficulty (11 percent of the sample were in this category). The analysis was a hierarchical, computerized clustering procedure (Shepard and others, 1983). Some of the results were as follows: Ten percent of the sample had handicaps other than learning disabilities (such as retardation), 6 percent were more validly classified as problems of language interference rather than learning disability, 10 percent were normal, and around 40 percent had reliable signs of learning disabilities, by the conventional criteria. The latter finding resulted in a front-page headline that asserted that half of the Colorado handicapped were misidentified.

The prevalence study verified that the trend in rates was rapidly upward and that rates differed among school districts by an astonishing amount. The cost analysis revealed that the costs of identification equaled the cost of treatment. The tests used to diagnose learning disabilities failed to meet professional standards. The identification procedures satisfied regulations but were excessive (the typical child received 6.6 tests and was diagnosed by 7.6 different professionals). The survey of these professionals showed their satisfaction with their own procedures, inability to discriminate good tests from poor ones, and admission that parents were sometimes intimidated by the role of professionals in decision making.

The Qualitative Side. Two hundred of the pupil cases were photocopied and qualitatively analyzed using the constant comparative method (Glaser and Strauss, 1967). Among the categories derived from the data were "cluster," which paralleled the concept of cluster in the quantitative analysis, and "consistency," which reflected the pattern of diagnoses among professionals, whether professionals attended to similar characteristics of a pupil, whether multiple sources of data coalesced, and whether alternative explanations were considered and contradictions examined. Ultimately, the percentages of cases falling into these categories were computed. A quota sample of cases falling into conjunctive categories was selected and narrative case histories written (Smith, 1982).

Reflections on the Study. Triangulation of the qualitative and quantitative analyses was achieved, except that the category of emotional difficulties was much more salient in the qualitative analysis. However, the two forms of analysis were not independent in the strict sense, making this study more like the fifth than the fourth circumstance, described earlier. Because of anticipated controversy, we commissioned reactions to the study by multiple interest groups and included them in the final report (Shepard and Smith, 1981). In response to the study, the legislature conducted public hearings, task forces were appointed to propose solutions to the problem, and interest groups organized resistence. When the dust settled, policy makers made changes (described in Davis and Smith, 1984).

Another Example: The Kindergarten Retention Study

During 1983, the Boulder Valley Public Schools confronted a dilemma. In certain of its elementary schools, almost half of beginning pupils were being asked to spend two years in kindergarten. In other schools all children were promoted from kindergarten to first grade after only one year. The district has a tradition of relative school autonomy, yet such glaring differences among its schools were impossible to ignore. Coordination problems were apparent when families moved from one school attendance area to another. An active group of parents and professionals promoted the philosophy of the Gesell Institute, which advocates additional time for "developmentally young" children to mature prior to their placement in first grade. There was pressure on the administration of the district to expand the program of developmental or pre-kindergartens, at that time operating in two schools. This program involved diagnosis, with the Gesell School Readiness Test, of children entering kindergarten. Those who were diagnosed "developmentally young" were placed in a pre-kindergarten, at the end of one year of which they entered regular kindergarten.

Against this background, Shepard and I were asked to conduct a policy evaluation of practices related to two-year kindergarten programs (either through the formal pre-kindergarten programs or through the retention of an unsuccessful kindergartener for another year in regular kindergarten) and the effects of such programs on children. The study was commissioned by the department of elementary education. The principal audience was the early childhood education committee and the central administration and school board. The other stakeholding groups included pupils, parents, teachers, first-grade teachers, advocates and adversaries of the Gesell philosophy, and early childhood educators, generally.

Our experience with the Colorado Learning Disabilities Identification Study convinced us of the merits of combining qualitative and quantitative approaches. Because there were strong competing interests in this setting (retaining and nonretaining schools, pro- and anti-Gesellians, and the like), a solely qualitative design would not have been sufficiently persuasive, no matter what direction the results took. We needed the weight of authority provided by what Cronbach (1982) termed a *strong design.* The strongest design under the circumstances was a matched control group quasi-experiment (random assignment being neither feasible nor ethical).

Yet, we also believed that there must be some explanation for the great discrepancy among schools in their rates of retention in kindergarten. We had evidence that such rates could *not* be explained by differences in the economic position of the separate schools or in their average levels of ability and achievement. Therefore, we reasoned, differences might be explained by the educational and social contexts of the schools (what level of pupil expectations were held, how teaching was done, how parents, pupils, and teachers interacted with each other) or by the philosophies and beliefs held by teachers. The possibility of directly measuring teacher's beliefs through questionnaires was rejected because of reactivity of measurement. We proposed instead to conduct clinical interviews with the teachers and small case studies of selected kindergarten classes.

> **The Quantitative Side: What Are the Effects of Retention?** A quasi-experimental design with post-hoc matching was deemed to be the strongest possible test of the effects of retention. Random assignment of children to promoted or retained groups was not feasible, but conditions provided for a "natural experiment," since certain schools regularly retained a large percentage of kindergartners while others normally retained a small percentage. Three schools with high rates of retention were matched with three other schools having low rates of retention. Matching variables included a percent of the population receiving free lunches, average standardized test scores, and size. Within these schools, pupils were selected in matched pairs, one from a high-retaining school who had experienced two years of kindergarten, and one from a low-retaining school who had experienced only one year of kindergarten. The matching variables were age (by month) at which they entered kindergarten, sex, socioeconomic status, native language, and various entrance test scores.

Effects of the two kindergarten conditions were measured at the end of the children's first-grade year with a variety of instruments. Standardized tests (California Test of Basic Skills) were routinely administered to all children during the spring and yielded reading and math scores. In addition, we prepared teacher rating forms so that the children's first-grade teachers could assess reading and math achievement, social maturity, learning self-concept, and appropriate attention to school work. The teachers rated the children both in relation to grade-level standards and in comparison with peers. In addition, telephone interviews with parents yielded parents' assessments of their children's progress in school subjects, attitude about school, peer relationships, and readiness for second grade. No matter which angle the data were examined from, the results of the quasi-experiment demonstrated the lack of efficacy of spending two years in kindergarten. On all but one of the twelve measures of effect, the nonretained group was performing at the same level as those who had spent two years in kindergarten. Only on the CTBS reading subtest was there any advantage for the retained group, and that constituted only seven percentile ranks or one-month grade equivalent score over the average of the nonretained group. In terms of costs, the retained group had spent one additional year of schooling at a cost of about $3000 per student, with very little gain in academic performance or social maturity. The findings from this study are consistent with the research on retention (Holmes and Matthews, 1984; Gredler, 1984).

The Qualitative Side: What Is the Meaning of Retention and How Does It Happen? Parent Interviews. In addition to the rating scales administered to parents during telephone interviews, a series of open-ended questions were also posed. The purpose of these was to document from the parents' point of view the processes of retention and promotion and the interactions between the school and the family about this decision. In an indirect and nonreactive way, we sought to uncover the opinions parents held. The data were analyzed with some techniques adapted from Miles and Huberman (1984) and summarized within temporal categories; for example, opinions held about children's readiness for school prior to kindergarten, during kindergarten, during the time when the decision was made to retain or promote, and at the end of first grade. Within a category, such as progress at the end of first grade, opinions were ordered along a dimension of positive to negative perceptions. Statements from interviews were then selected to depict points along the dimension. The purpose of this analysis was to understand and communicate the variability of opinions and reported experiences. The following excerpts from interviews of two parents were selected to represent opinions about the decision to retain two children.

> The teachers first suggested that he repeat. I saw that he had no interest in reading and he couldn't stay in one place long enough. They said that he should go through kindergarten again because he just wasn't mature enough, although he could do the [academic] work. I discussed it with him. I didn't want to hold him back without him being aware of what was happening. I told him, "you know, you're not doing real well in school, you're not ready to go on." He couldn't read very well to me. He could pick out just words or guess by looking at the picture what the story was about. I told him, "what do you think, if I hold you back, will that bother you?" He said, "No." I probably would have done it anyway because it was the best thing for him. He seemed to accept it.

> It was in January. They called me in, and at the time they hadn't said it was something really serious or my husband would

have gone in. It was both teachers and principal telling me that behaviorally and socially he was behind, and they felt that he needed some more time in the kindergarten situation to catch up with the other children. And again, they said academically he was fine. It was just that in those other areas he was about six months behind. I had a lot of feelings. I was sure at that time that they were mistaken about him. I was just so shocked. You think everything is all right, then all of a sudden you find out it isn't, especially with your first child. I didn't take it too well. I got really upset. Not having my husband there and feeling really outnumbered three-to-one was really intimidating to me. Later, he went through some [Gesell] testing, some kind of developmental test. The psychologist said he wasn't ready for first and suggested a transition program. We tried to get him in one, but couldn't. At the end of the summer we had to make a decision, so we just went along with what everybody told us and had him repeat kindergarten. We learned to live with it, but looking at him now—he still has some behavioral problems—makes me wonder whether anything was gained.

Though difficult to summarize, the data from parents of children who were retained were variable. The parents believed that more good than harm had come about as a result of retention. Yet they also reported that psychological adjustments to the decision had to be made, that many retained children perceived themselves to be failures, that there were conflicts among family members and between the family and the school regarding the decision, and the like. The parents of children who had been recommended for retention but who resisted this recommendation portrayed considerable conflicts about the decision (yet the children apparently suffered few consequences of being promoted against the school's recommendation). Parents of promoted children (matched on pre-kindergarten characteristics with retained children) had never even considered the possibility that their children might not be ready for first grade. The idea of retention had simply never entered their consciousness. What these parents had not known apparently had not hurt their children.

Teacher Interviews. Thirty-nine of the forty-four kindergarten teachers in the district were interviewed by myself using indirect and nonreactive methods. Some categories of information were specified in advance, including the characteristics teachers react to when they decide whether a child is ready for school, their beliefs about child development, and what the teacher can do for the child who is poorly prepared for first grade. Interviews were recorded and transcribed. The verbatim transcriptions were content-analyzed using a scheme of qualitative analysis. In addition to the forty categories of information that were specified at the beginning of analysis, several categories were extracted from the data. One of these was the idea of "downward pressure," the curriculum of later grades (for example, teaching vowel sounds) being expected of kindergarten teachers.

The report on the teacher interviews centered on three issues of overriding importance—the diversity of teacher beliefs, teacher perceptions of the merits of retention, and pressures on kindergarten teachers. The marked variation among teachers in their beliefs about how children develop readiness for school was obvious in the interviews but difficult to portray. Through a largely inductive process, I decided that teachers' beliefs could be ordered along a continuum of nativism to environmentalism. That is, there were some teachers who believed that the mechanisms that govern a child's developing readiness for school are internal: physiological and psychological. Others believed that those mechanisms were external: social and instructional (development can be influenced by intervening in a child's environment or by teaching him or her something). A display was created to show how each teacher might be situated on this continuum. A further dimension was suggested by differences among the teachers in their response to children they regard as unprepared for school. The two categories were shown to be related and were shown together on a two-dimensional display. In juxtaposing the two dimensions, one could see four clusters of teachers. Excerpts from the transcripts of these four sets of teachers were organized to show how remarkably diverse their beliefs were. Paraphrases of the excerpts were written in an attempt to reduce the sheer amount of data to a manageable amount, without losing the true meaning of the raw data. The following paraphrases illustrate beliefs about development held by two of the four clusters of teachers.

Beliefs About What the Teacher Can Do for the
Unready Child

Cluster One. "Teachers can provide children with more time to mature; place children in developmental kindergarten, preschool, send them home another year, place them in the slow group in class, reduce instruction below frustration level, lower expectations, boost self-concept, use manipulatives to teach concepts at the psychomotor level, then retain them in kindergarten or place in transition room—providing academic assistance is irrelevant and harmful."

Cluster Four. "Teachers can provide additional academic help, accommodate differences in achievement, hold high expectations, reinforce, and train—work hard and encourage the pupil to work hard."

The two-dimensional display was used to demonstrate the relationship between teacher beliefs and retention practices. Teachers who believed that children's readiness develops through an organic unfolding process with little impact from the environment also tended to be those who retained a large percentage for a second year in kindergarten. Diversity of beliefs was also found to be related to the school. That is, with only a few exceptions, teachers in the same school shared beliefs about development.

In contrast to the diversity of teachers' beliefs about development, there was virtual unanimity in beliefs about the positive effects of retention. This was true whether the teacher retained many or none or what cluster of beliefs the treacher typified. No one felt there were any deleterious effects of spending two years in kindergarten, although some believed that placement into a two-year, developmental kindergarten was preferable to retention. Most felt that a child who spent an extra year in kindergarten would move from the bottom of his or her class to the top of the class into which he or she was retained.

The pressures on the kindergarten teacher were evident from the interviews. Children who are held out of kindergarten until age six are mixed into classes who enter at the legal age of five. Many entering kindergarteners are already able to read. But because others are not, the class is grossly heterogeneous. First-grade teachers in some schools insist that children are ready to start their reading primers on the first day of school. This makes it necessary for the kindergarten teachers to push for mastery of prereading skills. Parents in this district also push for an orientation on academics rather than on socialization.

Case Studies. Short-term case studies were conducted on three high-retaining, three low-retaining, and one pre-kindergarten. The purpose of this part of the study was to describe the classes and attempt to discover any differences in the curriculum or instruction in the schools. The studies were naturalistic in the sense that categories and propositions were not defined in advance of data collection. What was documented by the case studies was that the differences in rates of retention could not be explained by any obvious variation in quality of instruction, effectiveness of teachers, or curriculum. All classes except the pre-kindergarten were found to be efficient, fast-paced and academically oriented kindergartens. There was the suggestion that, in the high-retaining schools, the expectations held for children believed to be immature were lower than those held for other children. But the brevity of the studies (about twenty hours apiece) made this interpretation equivocal.

Reflections on the Study. The long, complicated report (Shepard and Smith, 1985) was presented orally and in various forms to as many audiences as could be summoned. Despite our attempts to emphasize the philosophical and contextual findings in the qualitative studies, which we felt explained retention practices, most audiences responded to the quantitative outcomes. The disparity between the beliefs of some teachers and administrators about the efficacy of retention and the negative results of the quantitative study inevitably led to controversy. Those who had held anti-Gesellian views before the study were quiet while loud protests were heard from the other side. However, the comprehensiveness of the study as a whole and the rigor with which it was conducted all but eliminated objections to its methodology. District administrators were reluctant to issue a central policy about retention, yet they eliminated the two-year pre-kindergarten programs.

On reflection, we feel that this study best fits the first, third, fourth, and sixth circumstances described at the beginning of this chapter. Contextual description of classroom processes and teacher beliefs illuminated the contrasting treatments, lent authenticity, and provided a partial explanation for how things were. The case studies were targeted and selection of cases interpretable. However, the categories that we felt at the end of the study were the most important, such as "downward pressure" and "view of first grade," were not known in advance and therefore were not the objects of study. Triangulation was a desired outcome, yet it was only partly achieved. Multimethod assessments of the outcomes of retention corroborated each other but conflicted with teachers' perceptions of the merits of retention. Falling short of triangulation was probably the result of our decision to proceed inductively in the qualitative studies. Doing otherwise would have blinded us to what seems now to be our most important, though tentative interpretation—that the urge to retain may be a response to ever-increasing heterogeneous classroom composition and greater demands for mastery of reading skills.

However, the case studies contributed less than they might have if they had been focused on categories discovered in other parts of the study. In other words, a serial design would have been preferable to a simultaneous one. The information needs of different audiences were attended to, although it is clear from examining the excerpts from parent interviews that qualitative data present a dilemma. They are concrete and real and offering them untreated is the only way to convey the opinions held by these individuals. Yet reporting them requires space and demands reader investment, perhaps more than can be reasonably expected. They are also more apt to be criticized because they are inherently personal (hence viewed as subjective or false) and selectively reported. Perhaps advances in methodology on the order of Miles and Huberman (1984) are required before dilemmas such as these can be solved.

Conclusion

It is clear by now what my preferences are. I know the objections. Combining qualitative and quantitative approaches costs too much, pits paradigms against each other, requires skills that do not coalesce in many individuals and sometimes do not even reside hospitably on the same research team, and so on. But the merits outweigh the difficulties if the evaluator is ingenious and eager to make the best of the kinds of circumstances described here.

The coherent use of historical analysis, life history,
and ethnographic observation is illustrated.

Qualitative Research and Evaluation: Triangulation and Multimethods Reconsidered

Louis M. Smith
Paul F. Kleine

In this chapter we raise several conceptual issues in the theory of evaluation methodology and illustrate them with items from our recent study, *Kensington Revisited: A Fifteen-Year Follow-Up of an Innovative School and Its Faculty* (Smith and others, 1984). First, and mostly by way of assumption, we would like to narrow, if not dissolve, the distinction between research and evaluation. In our view the recent discussions and debates on the nature of paradigms in social science and education make the distinction tenuous, if not untenable (Fay, 1975; Bernstein, 1978; Bredo and Feinberg, 1982). In our view, neither research nor evaluation is value free. Second, we would like to extend the range of what is usually considered the scope of triangulation and multimethods as they have been discussed by Denzin (1970), Campbell and Fiske (1959), and Smith (1979). Essentially, we do this by focusing on three qualitative methods—ethnography, history, and biography or life history. Third, we approach the problems concretely, that is,

D. D. Williams (Ed.). *Naturalistic Evaluation.*
New Directions for Program Evaluation, no. 30. San Francisco: Jossey-Bass, June 1986.

with extended data and interpretations from the Kensington Revisited project. Finally, we structure our discussion, in part, as a story of what happened to us as researchers in the course of doing the project.

Briefly, the Kensington Revisited study involved returning to the site of our earlier ethnographic investigation, as described in *Anatomy of Educational Innovation* (Smith and Keith, 1971), in which we described and analyzed the problems of an innovative elementary school beginning its first year. Now, fifteen years later, we were looking for the mid- to long-term consequences of innovation. Our strategy seemed simple: Go back to the school and find the original faculty, have a look and a series of conversations, and note what had been happening in the interim. Actually, it was a bit more complicated than that. We were fortunate in receiving substantial resources through the National Institute of Education, from the newly formulated program on organizational processes in education. Instead of "progressively focusing," the project grew and grew. Ultimately, the final report reached six book-length volumes. We were several years overdue in finishing the NIE contract. The growing pains reflected a series of unanticipated events as the project got underway. When we first returned to the building, among a number of items, we found that the school population had changed from being 100 percent white to 40 percent white and 60 percent black. Our follow-up study of innovation was awash in much broader social change.

In the very first interview with one of the original Kensington faculty members, who has now retired, she commented on how she had first taught in the Marquette School, which was a part of another district before it had been annexed into the Milford School District in the late 1940s, and she talked of a small black school that had been in existence for years in the district. We found we could not understand the particulars of her career pattern without finding out considerably more about the history of the district. Shortly thereafter we found a file of newsletters that the district sent to patrons. They had begun in 1952. In reading them in the curriculum room located in the Milford District central office, we came on what looked like a muted but serious conflict between the board and the then superintendent, Mr. McBride. One day as the current superintendent, Dr. Ronald George, walked by, we raised the issue with him. He commented that it had been a terrible time for Superintendent McBride. After a few minutes of conversation he wandered off, only to return shortly with a large black bound book. This was our first view of the "Minutes" of the Milford School Board. He opened them to the meeting in which the president of the board had read off a long list of particulars on the inadequacies of Superintendent McBride. The board president concluded by calling for a vote demanding McBride's resignation. Beyond the substantive issues surrounding McBride's problems, the methodological issues of historical data sources immediately became entrancing. To questions about other volumes of minutes and their availability to us, Superintendent George indicated that he had a closet full and we were welcome to have a look. That closet full of minutes ran back to approximately 1915. Reading them added two years to the project's life.

The farther we went down these interrelated paths, the more convinced we were of their importance and the more we felt a need to rationalize them. We believe that ethnography, history, and biography or life history are three powerful qualitative methods that triangulate in ways much larger in scope than we would have guessed from accounts presented in the provocative and well-received statements by Denzin (1970) and Campbell and Fiske (1959) or in accounts of our earlier attempts to integrate them into our work (Smith and Pohland, 1974, and Smith, 1979). We couple this rationale with a distinction of Scrive's (1966) regarding criticism and evaluation in the arts. He speaks of "elucidatory criticism" and "evaluative criticism." The former tries to clarify the lay of the land while the latter often attempts to develop comparative statements and criterion statements. Each claim, elucidatory or evaluative, requires justification until a rationale or web of statements and reasons is built. Our task as educational evaluators and researchers, we believe, is similar. The substantive theme, along with its interconnected web of statements that we wish to follow in this analysis, is that of innovation in schooling. In particular we are concerned with the position of superintendent, both the role and the incumbent, in relation to the establishment of an innovative school. The multimethods of ethnography, history, and life history present different images for understanding. Such triangulation achieves a potency rarely accomplished in educational research and evaluation.

Images of Superintendent Steven Spanman

An Early View. In our initial view of Superintendent Spanman, we knew him as the man who had invited us into the school district to do the research that became *Anatomy of Educational Innovation* (Smith and Keith, 1971). In this regard he gave us both freedom and support to proceed as our best judgment directed. He garnered some district funds, and he helped us obtain a small grant from the Office of Education. He was the man who had conceived the idea of an innovative school, sought out an architect to design the open-space building, and initiated the mandate to the faculty, "Go build a school," regarding its curriculum and instructional program. He was also one of several who sent a child to the school. Finally, we saw him as looking and acting like an evangelist. Some of our colleagues across the country who had known him in other contexts had a considerably less favorable image than these items represent.

Images from the Historical Record. A new era began in the Milford School District in the summer of 1962. Dr. Steven Spanman was now superintendent. He had not arrived for the July school board meeting. Business was attended to as usual. The only directives to Dr. Spanman noted in the board minutes concerned enrollment. Dr. Spanman was to contact the superintendent of the Catholic Diocesan Schools to "ascertain the enrollment plans in the elementary schools for the next three years, as it would affect the Milford School District," and to "submit a complete report and recommendations of the projected enrollment patterns and the area need for school building programs." What was to become the Kensington School was in the offing. A memo existed on the purchasing of lots for a building site. A letter from a local architectural firm, which had designed the recently built Hillside School, indicated its desire to design any new schools, possibly adapting an existing plan.

The new superintendent was present at the August 28 meeting. The agenda was long and the minutes were full of items carrying the phrase "as recommended by the superintendent." Each item passed unanimously. Perhaps our knowledge of Superintendent Spanman clouded our views, but we believe anyone reading the minutes would have come away with a feeling that an active, take-charge individual was the new incumbent in the superintendent position. The superintendent's mimeographed "Agenda" was now enclosed with the minutes "for purposes of reference." Twenty-six items were elaborated in the twenty-three-page, typed single-spaced statement. Our intent is to explore this first meeting in some detail, for it seems to capture much of Spanman's personality, perspective, and administrative style.

The Content of the First Agenda. Item by item, the content varied in importance and breadth of impact. Item one dealt with a longstanding inequity in Suburban County's tax rate. The board was urged to go on record in support of the attempt for equalization. Milford, as one of the larger and less wealthy districts, would profit thereby. With his recommendation, Spanman moved directly into a major issue in Suburban County, equalization of resources for the schools. Beyond the content itself, we are left with an image of Spanman's ability as a "quick study." During our ethnographic investigation, casual conversations and interviews with central office personnel reveal perceptions such as "brilliant" and "imaginative."

Item two dealt with the organization of the administrative and supervisory staff. The assistant superintendent and business officials who had been reporting directly to the board ever since the conflict between the board and former Superintendent McBride were now to report to the superintendent. For all the noises about "democracy" in the Kensington School, and that had been a real and important issue (see Smith and Keith, 1971, Chapter Eight), Spanman's action at the district level made it very clear that he was to be the center of power and communication.

Item four was an invitation extended to the Metropolitan Superintendents' Association for the fall meeting to be held at the new Milford Junior High School. "This item is for information," read the minutes. Spanman seemed to be testing the local superintendency waters. Superintendents were invited to his turf and to see Milford's Junior High School. At a minimum, the inference was that he moved quickly in contacts with his peers.

Item six responded to the request of a parent to have his son admitted to first grade. The problem involved an October 12 birthdate; school policy required the child to be six on or before September 15th. The extenuating circumstances were a move from another community where the child had had six months of nursery school, a full year of kindergarten, and a recommendation for promotion to first grade. The superintendent recommended that the parents' request be denied. These realities contrasted sharply with the idealism later articulated at Kensington in its ultimate goals of individualization as to entrance, graduation, hours of daily attendance, and days of yearly attendance (Smith and Keith, 1971).

Item eight reported on a meeting between Spanman and the superintendent of the Archdiocesan Schools: "The meeting was very profitable and beneficial." The Milford community had always had a large parochial population. At a prior meeting of the board, members had directed the superintendent to inquire regarding enrollment projections. He responded immediately. Item nine was a request by the superintendent to permit his acceptance of an invitation to make an audiovisual presentation, "at no expense to the district," to a seminar of "a most interesting and especially well-informed cross-section of military, academic, governmental, and industrial personnel." Dr. Spanman, as we came to see, was both an engaging lecturer and a proponent of technology in the schools. National exposure was a part of his continuing agenda. Cosmopolitanism was part of his style. Technological innovations, in his view, were part of the promise of education's future.

Item ten, consultant services of the Architectual Design Institute (ADI), played directly into what was to become the Kensington School and extended our understanding of the organizational and administrative roots of educational innovation: Consequently, we reproduce part of the several paragraphs from the superintendent's agenda.

> Dr. James Holland, director of the Architectual Design Institute, has indicated that he and his staff are interested in giving assistance in school planning for the Milford School District. . . .

> The Architectural Design Institute is interested in school systems searching for new knowledge and wishes to leave to others who have more money (like the federal government) to help people who have no ideas. Many new ideas are currently under investigation by the district's curriculum study. . . .

The Architectural Design Institute would provide the much desired consultant services for assisting the staff in determining the educational specifications from which the most efficient architectual plans could be developed for the proposed Kensington Elementary School. . . .

The new superintendent was moving the district into contact with national organizations, resources, and ideas. The second paragraph presents an item suggesting hypotheses of both an elitism and an antifederal government perspective.

Item eleven, progress on the language laboratory, seemed to carry multiple messages as well.

Upon their return from vacation during the first week of August, members of the administrative staff were greatly disappointed that very little work had been done on the Language Laboratory during the month of July. . . .

A representative of National Technology Corporation met with members of the administrative staff and informed them that the earliest possible completion date would be September 4. The company was again informed of the school district's position. After a phone conversation with his general manager, the company representative assured the school district that the laboratory would be completed no later than August 27. . . .

"A shaker and a mover" is another label that has remained part of Spanman's reputation with Milford School District personnel. Lurking behind the label was a sense of efficacy, a view that the education world was malleable through his efforts. We find ourselves reaching beyond the historical data for inferences related to other conversations, observations, and experiences. We insert them along the way to elaborate the evolving profile. Multimethods and triangulation continue at several levels of generality.

Item eighteen, employment of architect, and items nineteen and twenty concerning the school site for Kensington fall together. The parcels of land were being accumulated lot by lot. The move toward the selection of the architect was a part of a larger strategy.

Considerable amount of educational planning must be done by the administrative and supervisory staff before an architect is engaged to design the building for the Kensington Elementary School. It is the opinion of the staff that obtaining the services of an architect as a first step toward the acquisition of a new building is a mistake. An architect should be engaged only after the staff and the board know exactly what educational program it wishes to offer the children and what spaces are needed to house the program. It is at this point that the talents of an architect can be utilized most advantageously. The more information the architect is given in the form of educational specifications, the better job he or she can do toward satisfying the educational needs of the pupils served by the school. The Architectural Design Institute (assuming approval of the recommendation submitted in item ten) will assist the staff in determining the educational specifications.

The superintendent presented an explicit procedure for selecting an architect—publicizing the district's intent, initial screening by administrative staff, final evaluation and selection by the board. Almost for the first time, education—the curriculum, the goals, and the content—were to be taken as problematic. Prior to this an unquestioned consensus seemed to exist as conventional wisdom in the Milford community. Buildings followed "naturally" on that wisdom. In our effort to understand innovation and change, we have been struck with the importance "of what one makes problematic."

Item twenty-four dealt with "real estate development: its implications for future school planning." Discussion specifically focused on the Islington Apartments. Already 32 elementary-age pupils lived in 80 rented apartments, 190 units were completed, another 30 were to be ready for Christmas, and 440 would be the final total. A survey of 10 developers indicated that 702 additional school-age youngsters would appear. Demographic changes were continuing apace.

The Structure of the Agenda. First, the materials were organized and well written. Each point was made in a topic sentence or short paragraph. The next paragraph or two spelled out the subissues involved. In an important sense, one might infer that the superintendent was educating his board with clear, concise well-reasoned items. Second, each item culminated in a recommendation. The board was to go on record to take quite specific action. Discussions were background reasons and arguments. They were not idle chatter. They led to actions that were to improve the education of the youngsters of Milford. Concepts such as practical reasoning and theory of action spring out at the reader. Third, the comprehensiveness of the agenda, the quantity of issues, and the detail were overwhelming. For a board member to disagree would take considerable study, strength of character, and intellect. The superintendent was creating an image of strength and power, of a man who knew what he wanted and knew how to get it. Fourth, the superintendent was opening up relationships with the many facets, positions, and organizations of his world. These included the other superintendents, the archdiocesan schools, and national corporations supplying new educational technology. He was going to be centrally involved. Fifth, those social scientists who focus on interaction would discern that the origin or initiation of interaction had an exemplar in Spanman. Clearly he was in charge of administration within the District.

Images from a Life History. In the course of our study, we had a chance to spend several hours talking with Steven Spanman. In tha life history interview we learned a number of things about his background. These we integrated with other items and perspectives. In everyone's eyes, Steven Spanman had been a man on the move. It is tempting to say that rapidity of movement was the most salient dimension of Spanman's career. Born in a small southwestern town, he graduated from high school at seventeen, entered a Baptist college for a year, moved to a branch of the state university, and graduated at twenty. By twenty-four, he had completed two years of military service, received a master's in educational administration, and spent another year teaching. In the next five years he had finished two stints as a principal, completed an Ed.D., and become assistant superintendent in a city school district. At thirty-two he arrived in Milford. The fourth year of that tenure he took a leave of absence. After several years of foundation activity, at thirty-eight he became superintendent of a major city school system. After a decade of that he moved to a university professorship at Southwestern State University. Both of these later appointments involved a return to the state in which he had been born and raised.

Along the way several themes appeared that clarified the rapid career rise. Related, presumably antecedent to, rapid upward mobility were high energy and high activity levels:

> *Interviewer.* Did you go right on to State University Branch, then, out of high school?
> *Steve Spanman.* Well now, when I graduated high school, I went to the Baptist College, junior college, one year, on a football scholarship. The reason is the coach from our little conference down there went up there as head coach. And he wanted me to come up there. And then the second year I moved down to the State University Branch, which was a new school just started, and I went down there on a football scholarship. I played football and basketball.
> *Int.* All the way through college?
> *SS.* Well, yeah, I graduated in thirty months.
> *Int.* From the junior college?
> *SS.* Yeah, I really didn't have my senior year. I graduated, I walked across the stage when I was nineteen, but I guess I was twenty in June.

Playing two major sports on an athletic scholarship and finishing college in less than three years, just before he reached twenty, demands a number of talents, one of which is energy.

A second theme appears in the form of ambition, sponsorship, prestigious schools of education, and the network of education administration in the United States. By attending Eastern University for his Ed.D., Spanman broke into a small prestigious community of educational administration. That group recruited, trained, and placed able young professionals. Furthermore, the group members consulted with boards in various ways. The network was broadly located across the country. It had its own norms and beliefs about education, administration, and careers. A brief comment from Spanman about the Milford School District suggests some of these elements and interrelationships:

> *SS.* They were hired by the Milford board to select, to screen the superintendent applicants. They came to me and asked me if I would be interested in being considered. In their conversations with me they said it would be a good job for somebody for two to three years.
> *Int.* They phrased it that way to you?
> *SS.* Yeah, it was a . . . I was thirty-two when I went there. They said it would be good for my portfolio. Having been an Eastern University graduate, as you know, you go somewhere three years and you move. They said that the school board had taken the key away from the superintendent. And probably given that kind of a setting, you would be chopped up. That is usually what happens to a superintendent when he succeeds somebody who has been around twenty-seven years. McBride had been there for twenty-seven years, had grown up with it, and they explained that the old timers and the newcomers, and all of that bit. Well, the board, the newcomers, had taken over the board at that point. They said while there would be a lot of give and take, that that would be a good assignment for me, and that I ought to go there for two to three years, and be ready to move. Well, I did, I went there for two to three years, and sure enough I was ready to move [Taped interview, 1980].

Our point here is relatively simple, but profoundly important. To understand the innovation that was Kensington, one must understand Spanman the superintendent. To understand him, one must understand one of his key reference groups, the select network or community of educational administration that he had joined recently. Interpretively, the reader might move into a consideration of careerism, values, and inferences regarding the role of university mentors in the lives of young educationists.

The interviewers elected to pick up on the collegial network within school administration. Spanman presented his perspective and set of beliefs couched in the informal language of the network.

> *Int.* Talk a little about that network of which Eastern University and Washington, D.C., are obviously part of an access of some kind.

The Donaldsons and the . . . .

SS. At that time, Jones and Donaldson. It is Professor Wilson now, Thompson at Western and his predecessor, and whoever it was at Midwestern, pretty much controlled the big cities. They placed half of the big city superintendents, and right now Wilson is taking their place. He was superintendent in New York and has retired this last year from the university. He is a head hunter, and he works. For instance, I worked with him in selecting the Small City superintendent, and since then he has been on the selection committee. He was on the Southwestern City and four other selection committees across the country. That is the way it works.

Our earlier account of Spanman at the Kensington School (Smith and Keith, 1971) and our description and analysis from the "Board Minutes" indicates Spanman's strong interest in and commitment to technological solutions to educational problems emanating from American business enterprise. His earlier fascination and cathexis on overhead projectors and educational television had now shifted to computers. In addition to the strong technological flavor of the following paragraphs, the equally strong belief in radical solutions to educational problems coupled with the commitment to help the poorer children of our society is highly reminiscent of Spanman's earlier stance in Milford.

SS. Yeah, you see, unfortunately the computer will teach far better, some better than even the best teacher, and because it will be individualized, then there won't be any way to hold back the able student, and because the middle class influence will have access to it and some of the lower class families will not, that means that society will have to mount a massive effort to have equality.
. . .In 1990 the computer will be three times as productive as what you see in there, at half the cost. Simply, the way things are going we are going to become a more balanced industry between labor and capital. Labor-intensive industries are not going to survive, and unless educators perceive this, then we are in trouble. So you will have a Kensington type of school with three or four master teachers, with four or five regular teachers, with a bunch of technology and aids.

Int. So in a sense that is part of the Kensington dream, the nerve center, which was a part of that school, which at that time was tape recorders and art and some TV. In a sense, the idea was fifteen or twenty years ahead of its time, and partly lacked the key computer component.

SS. That is right. It is wired, and that school is designed to accommodate the micro and the network cable. See, at that school, you would have walls that are adjustable and at will and at once, you have got cables, runners, the whole thing. It would accommodate the micro.

Int. Still, now, after fifteen or twenty years.

SS. Yeah.

The absorption in the future, in new ideas, in the possibilities of technological breakthroughs, remained with Spanman. Spelling out visions, making myths, remained a large part of his creativity and charisma. These concerns were important not only as issues in beliefs about educational goals and educational means. In the context of the career analysis we were making, it was one more instance of Spanman placing himself on the "cutting edge," in the forefront of the educational action.

In conclusion, several key elements stand out. Spanman was and had been a bright, high-achieving, high-energy kind of man. His talent and energy took him early to prestigious Eastern University, where he found a national network of educational administrators. Spanman's comments are important here and they integrate with our more district-centered narrative on the historical and contemporaneous context of the Milford District. Conflict in the Milford District in 1961–62 was so severe that the board tried to fire Superintendent McBride. In a series of actions by the local C.T.A., the National Education Association Professional Affairs unit sent two investigators to Milford. One of their recommendations was to have several prestigious outside superintendents interview and screen candidates for a short list. One of these men was Dr. Macky, mentioned by Spanman in the interview.

From our other data, essentially superintendent agendas and school board minutes, we elaborate on the dimensions of proactive, cosmopolitan, imaginative educator and practical reasoner. None of these adjectives conflicts with the data presented here. In addition we spoke of Spanman's fascination with technology—then it was educational television and overhead projectors. Now later it was microcomputers. Underlying these is an early twentieth-century faith in technology solving basic problems of education and American society.

Adding Ethnographic Data: A Beginning Conceptualization of Spanman's Role as Innovator. Our first image involves such proactive descriptors as originating, initiating, leading out, taking charge. The contrast with reactive suggests making the world fit one's own categories, one's own needs, one's own purposes, rather than letting the world pose the problems, the definitions, and the solutions. Part of our proactive conception of Spanman is captured in the phrase "making things happen." Reading his board "agendas" from month to month captures the evolution of problems, analyses, and progressive, sequential action alternatives. Each one moves a step or two beyond the one before.

In Figure 1 we suggest some of the antecedents and consequences of the proactive stance. The cluster of characteristics that seem to describe Superintendent Spanman and that lurk behind the proactive role are elements of temperament, skill, and point of view. His high energy is reflected in comments by everyone we talked to. Central office personnel indicated he started early in the morning, had a late afternoon relief secretary, and often dictated memos late at night. Some thought he required only five or six hours of sleep. He exuded personal confidence, or efficacy, as it is sometimes called now. His professional life and rapid career rise provided personal testimony. Many in the district saw him as wrongly placed in Milford, a man on the move who would not stay long, who had a bigger professional agenda in mind. Nevertheless, while in Milford he devoted his talents to implementing his conception of excellence in schooling. Coupled with this point of view was an inexhaustible store of ideas; every problem had multiple facets, multiple alternatives, and multiple solutions. His verbal facility and persuasive skills are well caught in the homily reported by a Milford administrator, "He could talk the birds out of the trees."

The consequences we pinpoint here are simple. The intensity of work schedules he imposed on himself and others was severe. "You could see him coming, guess the size of the task, and know he would want it yesterday" is a paraphrase of a number of comments. Increased time and energy on professional tasks appeared everywhere in the system. Innovations occurred and the district changed. The proactive stance pervaded his relationships with everyone.

Spanman had a clear sense that new or additional work always required additional resources. He also had an array of possible institutions to be tapped for those resources. He seemed to have a flair for the game of a little here and a little there and leveraging a small amount from one place to gain more from a second or third. Further he seemed quite creative in staying in the spirit of the funds to make other things happen. For example, Architectural Design Institute monies to initiate travel across the state to the Thompson-built buildings were then supplemented by board monies. Similarly he piggy-backed on lecture funds with board funds to solicit additional funds for the building project. He was strongly supportive of our early research funding.

As we looked to the antecedents of "obtaining increased resources," a view of his proactive role and his personal efficacy reappeared. In addition, we perceived a dimension of cosmopolitanism. This seemed a mix of knowing places to go, knowing people when he got there, and meeting new people along the way. Long before Merton (1957) and Gouldner (1961) attacked the problem of cosmopolitanism, *Webster's* defined the concept simply, "Belonging to all the world; not local." Several letters attached to the minutes captured that flavor. The involvement outside the

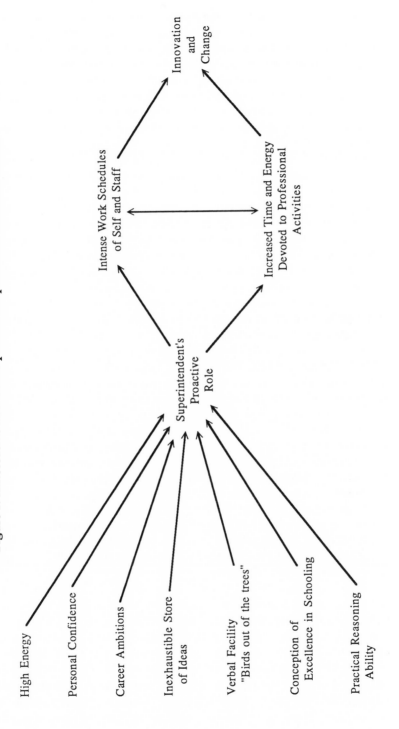

Figure 1: Antecedents and Consequences of Spanman's Proactive Stance

Milford District per se occurred at every level. He invited the county superintendents to Milford; he attended and frequently was on the program at
state and national educational meetings. He wandered afield with business,
government, and military groups and their representatives. He was actively
involved with national foundations and with university professors from
across the country. Early on, we, too, were a part of this (Smith and Keith,
1971). The contrasts in the flavor of this thinking and action from that of
his predecessor, McBride, who had been very much a localist, were sharp
and clear. He also contrasted with his successor, Dr. George.

Spanman was an imaginative educator. Here the accent lies on both
concepts—imaginative and educator. The most telling piece of evidence
was his approach to the problem of new buildings. The population data
indicated that the district was continuing to expand at the elementary
level. The Catholic parochial school plans had been tested initially during
a conversation with the Diocesan superintendent. A prior architect pressed
for continuation of their relationship. Spanman moved simply but directly
with the premise—the building must reflect the kind of educational programs desired for the children. Reading Spanman's agendas for the board
meetings is like listening to and talking with a good teacher. Each lesson
has a point, a cognitive context to engage the audience intellectually, and
a persuasive appeal to action.

Spanman seemed to have an unusual capacity to see and communicate drama in human events. On his return from an American Association
of School Administrators convention his report, submitted under the sig-
nature of the two board members, began with this introduction:

> In the five days of this convention representatives of the
> Board of Education had opportunities to take part in developing
> new ideas and charting the course for new directions in education
> in this community. For seventeen hours each day doors were open
> to new knowledge, new insights, and inspirations. . . . Participa-
> tion in this greatest of all conventions was an estimable value to
> the representatives. Without a doubt, the participation will bring
> inspiration, stimulation, and resourcefulness in making the pro-
> gram in the Milford School District as good as the best that any
> parents want for their child.

From overhead projectors to closed circuit television to computers,
Spanman possessed a deep and continuing fascination with the promise of
technology and a faith in the American entrepreneurial and business community. In the report on the AASA meeting, this paragraph appears as a
Section XI exhibit: "During the course of the convention, school representatives were privileged to spend many hours examining the fruits of the
initiative, ingenuity, and resourcefulness of American business firms; to
learn first-hand of the vast array of resources available for upgrading cur-

riculum and instruction. Some five hundred thirty exhibitors presented their wares in more than five acres of display space." A half-dozen of these exhibits would be directly related to the new Kensington School. We would also note again the potential of national conventions for influencing educational change and Spanman's continuing efforts to educate his board.

One of the issues lurking in our minds over the years has been the conception of practical reasoning (Walker, 1971; Schwab, 1969; Gauthier, 1967; Dewey, 1933). Spanman seemed to have been a practical reasoner par excellence. A few brief illustrations across several domains extend these ideas. In his agendas he seemed always to have specific goals in mind. Always there were things he wanted to do. Then he would talk all around the issue—reasons for wanting to do it, potential problems and difficulties, different ways of handling the main issue and the subsidiary ones—and finally all this would culminate in an action recommendations. At this point the board would begin its deliberations.

In social situations, as we inferred from the minutes and our interview, we found ourselves reacting and noting several clusters of activities that seemed part of practical reasoning. First, the kind of evidence Spanman responded to was often direct observation of events and conversations with knowledgeable participants in those events. Second, in reviewing and summarizing discussions there was always an accent on agreements that implied next steps. The conversations were always kept moving. Third, the discussions were always couched eventually in terms of specific concrete arrangements—dates, times, places, and individuals. The fuzziness of maybe or later or perhaps was not there.

A final illustration comes from Spanman's approach to curriculum problems. Typically the deliberations involved such questions as (1) What are we doing now—in reading, math, and so on? (2) What problems are we having? (3) What are some promising ideas and practices? and (4) How can we make them work to solve our problems? It was really the "promising ideas and practices" wording that caught our eye initially. The phrase could have been a cliché, but for Spanman it was a call to imagination, creativity, cosmopolitanism, enthusiasm, and making education better for the children in Milford's schools. In some sense, Dewey may have said all this years ago in his abstracted steps in problem solving. Perhaps all we are doing is painting a picture indicating this is one view of practical reasoning from the position of superintendent with an incumbent who has a special flair for innovation and change.

Conclusion

Our intent for this chapter was relatively simple and straightforward. By drawing on our recent project, *Kensington Revisited,* we hoped to illustrate and make an argument for several issues in naturalistic evaluation. First, powerful images of central actors in innovative educational projects can be developed from triangulating historical data, biographical life history data, and ethnographic data. Second, as the web or network of statements—factual, conceptual, and evaluative—is drawn in a particular context of time and place, readers are presented with a synthesized view, one that is similar to elucidatory and evaluative criticism in the arts. Third, as the readers prepare to engage in their own practical activity, for instance, in this case educational innovation, they can consider each item of "Spanman's experience" as it relates to their own personality, context, and decision making. How am I as "practical reasoner" or at "talking the birds out of the trees" persuasiveness? Am I following a prior superintendent of twenty-seven years' tenure who was "locked out" in a horrendous conflict with the school board? Do I have the kind of national contacts that permit me to make decisions about foundation support, architects, and consultants? Do I have a cosmopolitan old boys' network and a career line toward a large city superintendency or a professorship in educational administration?

In this chapter we deliberately chose to stay at a concrete, data level to make our case. An alternative would be the careful consideration of people, books, and ideas that we have found useful in rethinking and rationalizing our efforts (Smith, 1984; Smith and others, 1985). The two most provocative historical statements we found and used were Hexter's *A History Primer* (1971) and Stone's *The Past and Present* (1981). Concepts such as "second record" and "prosopography" have been fascinating points of departure for us. In the biographical, life history strand of our work it is Catherine Drinker Bowen's *Biography: The Craft and the Calling* (1968) and *Adventures of a Biographer* (1959), which have been so stimulating, even more than Langness and Frank's *Lives: An Anthropological Approach to Biography* (1981). Her essays leave one amazed and envious at her scholarly interest in biographical method and at her insights into the process itself. Perhaps better known to qualitative educational social scientists and evaluators are Geertz's two collections of essays, *Interpretation of Cultures* (1973) and *Local Knowledge* (1983). "Thick description" is well into contemporary literature and discussion; "blurred genres" and "common sense as a cultural system" soon will be. We believe the blending of ethnography, biography, and history is an important reconsideration and extension of the conceptions of triangulation and multimethods in naturalistic inquiry. If our argument is sound, it has implications for the educational community's norms as to what are legitimate methods of research and evaluation.

References

Bernstein, R. *The Restructuring of Social and Political Theory.* Philadelphia: University of Pennsylvania Press, 1978.
Bowen, C. D. *Adventures of a Biographer.* Boston: Little, Brown, 1959.
Bowen, C. D. *Biography: The Craft and the Calling.* Boston: Little, Brown, 1968.

Bredo, E., and Feinberg, W. (Eds.). *Knowledge and Values in Social and Educational Research*. Philadelphia: Temple University Press, 1982.

Campbell, D. T., and Fiske, D. W. "Convergent and Discriminant Validation by the Multitrait-Multimethod Matrix." *Psychological Bulletin*, 1959, *56*, 81–105.

Denzin, N. *The Research Act: A Theoretical Introduction to Sociological Methods*. Chicago: Aldine, 1970.

Dewey, J. *How We Think*. Chicago: Regnery, 1933.

Fay, B. *Social Theory and Political Practice*. London: George Allen and Unwin, 1975.

Gauthier, D. P. *Practical Reasoning*. New York: Oxford University Press, 1967.

Geertz, C. *The Interpretation of Cultures*. New York: Basic Books, 1973.

Geertz, C. *Local Knowledge: Further Essays in Interpretive Anthropology*. New York: Basic Books, 1983.

Gouldner, A. W. "Theoretical Requirements of the Applied Social Sciences." In W. Bennis and others (Eds.), *The Planning of Change*. New York: Holt, Rinehart & Winston, 1961.

Hexter, J. *The History Primer*. New York: Basic Books, 1971.

Langness, L. L., and Frank, G. *Lives: An Anthropological Approach to Biography*. Novato, Calif.: Chandler & Sharp, 1981.

Merton, R. K. *Social Theory and Social Structure*. (Rev. ed.) Glencoe, Ill.: Free Press, 1957.

Schwab, J. "The Practical: A Language for Curriculum." *School Review*, 1969, *78*, 1–23.

Scriven, M. *Primary Philosophy*. New York: McGraw-Hill, 1966.

Smith, L. M. "An Evolving Logic of Participant Observation, Educational Ethnography and Other Case Studies." *Review of Research in Education*, 1979, *6*, 316–377.

Smith, L. M. "Ethnographic and Historical Method in the Study of Schooling." In I. Goodson and S. Ball (Eds.), *Defining the Curriculum*. London: Falmer Press, 1984.

Smith, L. M., and Keith, P. *Anatomy of Educational Innovation*. New York: Wiley, 1971.

Smith, L. M., Klein, P., Prunty, J., and Dwyer, D. "Educational Innovators: A Decade and a Half Later." In S. Ball and I. Goodson (Eds.), *Teachers' Lives and Careers*. London: Falmer Press, 1985.

Smith, L. M., and Pohland, P. A. "Education, Technology and the Rural Highlands." In D. Sjogren (Ed.), *Four Evaluation Examples: Anthropological, Economic, Narrataive, and Portrayal*. Chicago: Rand McNally, 1974.

Smith, L. M., Prunty, J., Dwyer, D., and Klein, P. *Kensington Revisited: A Fifteen-Year Follow-Up of an Innovative School and Its Faculty* (Vol. 1-6). Washington, D.C.: National Institute of Education, 1984.

Stone, I. *The Past and the Present*. Boston: Routledge & Kegan Paul, 1981.

Walker, D. F. "A Naturalistic Model for Curriculum Development." *School Review*, 1971, *81*, 51–65.

Louis M. Smith is professor of education at Washington University in St. Louis, Missouri.

Paul F. Kleine is professor of education at the University of Oklahoma at Norman.

*The emergence of a new paradigm of inquiry
(naturalistic) has, unsurprisingly enough, led to a
demand for rigorous criteria that meet traditional
standards of inquiry. Two sets are suggested, one
of which, the "trustworthiness" criteria, parallels
conventional criteria, while the second, "authenticity"
criteria, is implied directly by new paradigm
assumptions.*

But Is It Rigorous? Trustworthiness and Authenticity in Naturalistic Evaluation

*Yvonna S. Lincoln,
Egon G. Guba*

Until very recently, program evaluation has been conducted almost exclusively under the assumptions of the conventional, scientific inquiry paradigm using (ideally) experimentally based methodologies and methods. Under such assumptions, a central concern for evaluation, which has been considered a variant of research and therefore subject to the same rules, has been how to maintain maximum rigor while departing from laboratory control to work in the "real" world.

The real-world conditions of social action programs have led to increasing relaxation of the rules of rigor, even to the extent of devising studies looser than quasi-experiments. Threats to rigor thus abound in

We are indebted to Judy Meloy, graduate student at Indiana University, who scoured the literature for references to fairness and who developed a working paper on which many of our ideas depend.

D. D. Williams (Ed.). *Naturalistic Evaluation.*
New Directions for Program Evaluation, no. 30. San Francisco: Jossey-Bass, June 1986.

sections explaining how, when, and under what conditions the evaluation was conducted so that the extent of departure from desired levels of rigor might be judged. Maintaining true experimental or even quasi-experimental designs, meeting the requirements of internal and external validity, devising valid and reliable instrumentation, probabilistically and representatively selecting subjects and assigning them randomly to treatments, and other requirements of sound procedure have often been impossible to meet in the world of schools and social action. Design problems aside, the ethics of treatment given and treatment withheld poses formidable problems in a litigious society (Lincoln and Guba, 1985b).

Given the sheer technical difficulties of trying to maintain rigor and given the proliferation of evaluation reports that conclude with that ubiquitous finding, "no significant differences," is it not surprising that the demand for new evaluation forms has increased. What is surprising—for all the disappointment with experimental designs—is the *continued* demand that new models must demonstrate the ability to meet the same impossible criteria! Evaluators and clients both have placed on new-paradigm evaluation (Guba and Lincoln, 1981; Lincoln and Guba, 1985a) the expectation that naturalistic evaluations must be rigorous in the conventional sense, despite the fact that the basic paradigm undergirding the evaluation approach has shifted.

Under traditional standards for rigor (which have remained largely unmet in past evaluations), clients and program funders ask whether naturalistic evaluations are not so subjective that they cannot be trusted. They ask what roles values and multiple realities can legitimately play in evaluations and whether a different team of evaluators might not arrive at entirely different conclusions and recommendations, operating perhaps from a different set of values. Thus, the rigor question continues to plague evaluators and clients alike, and much space and energy is again consumed in the evaluation report explaining how different and distinct paradigms call forth different evaluative questions, different issues, and entirely separate and distinct criteria for determining the reliability and authenticity—as opposed to rigor—of findings and recommendations.

Rigor in the Conventional Sense

The criteria used to test rigor in the conventional, scientific paradigm are well known. They include exploring the truth value of the inquiry or evaluation (internal validity), its applicability (external validity or generalizability), its consistency (reliability or replicability), and its neutrality (objectivity). These four criteria, when fulfilled, obviate problems of confounding, atypicality, instability, and bias, respectively, and they do so, also respectively, by the techniques of controlling or randomizing possible sources of confounding, representative sampling, replication, and insulation of the investigator (Guba, 1981; Lincoln and Guba, 1985a). In fact, to use a graceful old English cliché, the criteria are honored more in the breach than in the observance; evaluation is but a special and particularly public instance of the impossibility of fulfilling such methodological requirements.

Rigor in the Naturalistic Sense: Trustworthiness and Authenticity

Ontological, epistemological, and methodological differences between the conventional and naturalistic paradigms have been explicated elsewhere (Guba and Lincoln, 1981; Lincoln and Guba, 1985a; Lincoln and Guba, 1986; Guba and Lincoln, in press). Only a brief reminder about the axioms that undergird naturalistic and responsive evaluations is given here.

The axiom concerned with the nature of reality asserts that there is no single reality on which inquiry may converge, but rather there are multiple realities that are socially constructed, and that, when known more fully, tend to produce diverging inquiry. These multiple and constructed realities cannot be studied in pieces (as variables, for example), but only holistically, since the pieces are interrelated in such a way as to influence all other pieces. Moreover, the pieces are themselves sharply influenced by the nature of the immediate context.

The axiom concerned with the nature of "truth" statements demands that inquirers abandon the assumption that enduring, context-free truth statements—generalizations—can and should be sought. Rather, it asserts that all human behavior is time- and context-bound; this boundedness suggests that inquiry is incapable of producing nomothetic knowledge but instead only idiographic "working hypotheses" that relate to a given and specific context. Applications may be possible in other contexts, but they require a detailed comparison of the receiving contexts with the "thick description" it is the naturalistic inquirer's obligation to provide for the sending context.

The axiom concerned with the explanation of action asserts, contrary to the conventional assumption of causality, that action is explainable only in terms of multiple interacting factors, events, and processes that give shape to it and are part of it. The best an inquirer can do, naturalists assert, is to establish plausible inferences about the patterns and webs of such shaping in any given evaluation. Naturalists utilize the field study in part because it is the only way in which phenomena can be studied holistically and *in situ* in those natural contexts that shape them and are shaped by them.

The axiom concerned with the nature of the inquirer-respondent relationship rejects the notion that an inquirer can maintain an objective distance from the phenomena (including human behavior) being studied, suggesting instead that the relationship is one of mutual and simultaneous influence. The interactive nature of the relationship is prized, since it is only because of this feature that inquirers and respondents may fruitfully learn together. The relationship between researcher and respondent, when properly established, is one of respectful negotiation, joint control, and reciprocal learning.

The axiom concerned with the role of values in inquiry asserts that far from being value-free, inquiry is value-bound in a number of ways. These include the values of the inquirer (especially evident in evaluation, for example, in the description and judgment of the merit or worth of an evaluand), the choice of inquiry paradigm (whether conventional or naturealistic, for example), the choice of a substantive theory to guide an inquiry (for example, different kinds of data will be collected and different interpretations made in an evaluation of new reading series, depending on whether the evaluator follows a skills or a psycholinguistic reading theory), and contextual values (the values inhering in the context, and which, in evaluation, make a remarkable difference in how evaluation findings may be accepted and used). In addition, each of these four value sources will interact with all the others to produce value resonance or dissonance. To give one example, it would be equally absurd to evaluate a skills-oriented reading series naturalistically as it would to evaluate a psycholinguistic series conventionally because of the essential mismatch in assumptions underlying the reading theories and the inquiry paradigms.

It is at once clear, as Morgan (1983) has convincingly shown, that the criteria for judging an inquiry themselves stem from the underlying paradigm. Criteria developed from conventional axioms and rationally quite appropriate to conventional studies may be quite inappropriate and even irrelevant to naturalistic studies (and vice versa). When the naturalistic axioms just outlined were proposed, there followed a demand for developing rigorous criteria uniquely suited to the naturalistic approach. Two approaches for dealing with these issues have been followed.

Parallel Criteria of Trustworthiness. The first response (Guba, 1981; Lincoln and Guba, 1985a) was to devise criteria that parallel those of the conventional paradigm: internal validity, external validity, reliability, and objectivity. Given a dearth of knowledge about how to apply rigor in the naturalistic paradigm, using the conventional criteria as analogs or metaphoric counterparts was a possible and useful place to begin. Furthermore, developing such criteria built on the two-hundred-year experience of positivist social science.

These criteria are intended to respond to four basic questions (roughly, those concerned with truth value, applicability, consistency, and neutrality), and they can also be answered within naturalism's bounds, albeit in different terms. Thus, we have suggested credibility as an analog to internal validity, transferability as an analog to external validity, dependability as an analog to reliability, and confirmability as an analog to objectivity. We shall refer to these criteria as criteria of trustworthiness (itself a parallel to the term *rigor*).

Techniques appropriate either to increase the probability that these criteria can be met or to actually test the extent to which they have been met have been reasonably well explicated, most recently in Lincoln and Guba (1985a). They include:

For credibility:
- Prolonged engagement—lengthy and intensive contact with the phenomena (or respondents) in the field to assess possible sources of distortion and especially to identify saliencies in the situation
- Persistent observation—in-depth pursuit of those elements found to be especially salient through prolonged engagement
- Triangulation (cross-checking) of data—by use of different sources, methods, and at times, different investigators
- Peer debriefing—exposing oneself to a disinterested professional peer to "keep the inquirer honest," assist in developing working hypotheses, develop and test the emerging design, and obtain emotional catharsis
- Negative case analysis—the active search for negative instances relating to developing insights and adjusting the latter continuously until no further negative instances are found; assumes an assiduous search
- Member checks—the process of continuous, informal testing of information by soliciting reactions of respondents to the investigator's reconstruction of what he or she has been told or otherwise found out and to the constructions offered by other respondents or sources, and a terminal, formal testing of the final case report with a representative sample of stakeholders.

For transferability:
- Thick descriptive data—narrative developed about the context so that judgments about the degree of fit or similarity may be made by others who may wish to apply all or part of the findings elsewhere (although it is by no means clear how "thick" a thick description needs to be, as Hamilton, personal communication, 1984, has pointed out).

For dependability and confirmability:
- An external audit requiring both the establishment of an audit trail and the carrying out of an audit by a competent external, disinterested auditor (the process is described in detail in Lincoln and Guba, 1985a). That part of the audit that examines the process results in a dependability judgment, while that part concerned with the product (data and reconstructions) results in a confirmability judgment.

While much remains to be learned about the feasibility and utility of these parallel criteria, there can be little doubt that they represent a substantial advance in thinking about the rigor issue. Nevertheless, there are some major difficulties with them that call out for their augmentation with new criteria rooted in naturalism rather than simply paralleling those rooted in positivism.

First, the parallel criteria cannot be thought of as a complete set because they deal only with issues that loom important from a positivist construction. The positivist paradigm ignores or fails to take into account precisely those problems that have most plagued evaluation practice since the mid 1960s: multiple value structures, social pluralism, conflict rather than consensus, accountability demands, and the like. Indeed, the conventional criteria refer only to methodology and ignore the influence of context. They are able to do so because by definition conventional inquiry is objective and value-free.

Second, intuitively one suspects that if the positivist paradigm did not exist, other criteria might nevertheless be generated directly from naturalist assumptions. The philosophical and technical problem might be phrased thus: Given a relativist ontology and an interactive, value-bounded epistemology, what might be the nature of the criteria that ought to characterize a naturalistic inquiry? If we reserve the term *rigor* to refer to positivism's criteria and the term *reliability* to refer to naturalism's parallel criteria, we propose the term *authenticity* to refer to these new, embedded, intrinsic naturalistic criteria.

Unique Criteria of Authenticity. We must at once disclaim having solved this problem. What follows are simply some strong suggestions that appear to be worth following up at this time. One of us (Guba, 1981) referred to the earlier attempt to devise reliability criteria as "primitive"; the present attempt is perhaps even more aboriginal. Neither have we as yet been able to generate distinct techniques to test a given study for adherence to these criteria. The reader should therefore regard our discussion as speculative and, we hope, heuristic. We have been able to develop our ideas of the first criterion, fairness, in more detail than the other four; its longer discussion ought not to be understood as meaning, however, that fairness is very much more important than the others.

Fairness. If inquiry is value-bound, and if evaluators confront a situation of value-pluralism, it must be the case that different constructions will emerge from persons and groups with differing value systems. The task of the evaluation team is to expose and explicate these several, possibly conflicting, constructions and value structures (and of course, the evaluators themselves operate from some value framework).

Given all these differing constructions, and the conflicts that will almost certainly be generated from them by virtue of their being rooted in value differences, what can an evaluator do to ensure that they are presented, clarified, and honored in a balanced, even-handed way, a way that the several parties would agree is balanced and even-handed? How do evaluators go about their tasks in such a way that can, while not guaranteeing balance (since nothing can), at least enhance the probability that balance will be well approximated?

If every evaluation or inquiry serves some social agenda (and it invariably does), how can one conduct an evaluation to avoid, at least probabilistically, the possibility that certain values will be diminished (and their holders exploited) while others will be enhanced (and their holders advantaged)? The problem is that of trying to avoid empowering at the expense of impoverishing; all stakeholders should be empowered in some fashion at the conclusion of an evaluation, and all ideologies should have an equal chance of expression in the process of negotiating recommendations.

Fairness may be defined as a balanced view that presents all constructions and the values that undergird them. Achieving fairness may be accomplished by means of a two-part process. The first step in the provision of fairness or justice is the ascertaining and presentation of different value and belief systems represented by conflict over issues. Determination of the actual belief system that undergirds a position on any given issue is not always an easy task, but exploration of values when clear conflict is evident should be part of the data-gathering and data-analysis processes (especially during, for instance, the content analysis of individual interviews).

The second step in achieving the fairness criterion is the negotiation of recommendations and subsequent action, carried out with stakeholding groups or their representatives at the conclusion of the data-gathering, analysis, and interpretation stage of evaluation effort. These three stages are in any event simultaneous and interactive within the naturalistic paradigm. Negotiation has as its basis constant collaboration in the evaluative effort by all stakeholders; this involvement is continuous, fully informed (in the consensual sense), and operates between true peers. The agenda for this negotiation (the logical and inescapable conclusion of a true collaborative evaluation process), having been determined and bounded by all stakeholding groups, must be deliberated and resolved according to rules of fairness. Among the rules that can be specified, the following seem to be absolute minimum.

1. Negotiations must have the following characteristics:
    a. It must be open, that is, carried out in full view of the parties or their representatives with no closed sessions, secret codicils, or the like permitted.
    b. It must be carried out by equally skilled bargainers. In the real world it will almost always be the case that one or another group of bargainers will be the more skillful, but at

least each side must have access to bargainers of equal skill, whether they choose to use them or not. In some instances, the evaluator may have to act not only as mediator but as educator of those less skilled bargaining parties, offering additional advice and counsel that enhances their understanding of broader issues in the process of negotiation. We are aware that this comes close to an advocacy role, but we have already presumed that one task of the evaluator is to empower previously impoverished bargainers; this role should probably not cease at the negotiation stage of the evaluation.

    c. It must be carried out from equal positions of power. The power must be equal not only in principle but also in practice; the power to sue a large corporation in principle is very different from the power to sue it in practice, given the great disparity of resources, risk, and other factors, including, of course, more skillful and resource-heavy bargainers.

    d. It must be carried out under circumstances that allow all sides to possess equally complete information. There is no such animal, of course, as "complete information," but each side should have the same information, together with assistance as needed to be able to come to an equal understanding of it. Low levels of understanding are tantamount to lack of information.

    e. It must focus on all matters known to be relevant.

    f. It must be carried out in accordance with rules that were themselves the product of a pre-negotiation.

2. Fairness requires the availability of appellate mechanisms should one or another party believe that the rules are not being observed by some. These mechanisms are another of the products of the pre-negotiation process.

3. Fairness requires fully informed consent with respect to any evaluation procedures (see Lincoln and Guba, 1985a, and Lincoln and Guba, 1985b). This consent is obtained not only prior to an evaluation effort but is continually renegotiated and reaffirmed (formally with consent forms and informally through the establishment and maintenance of trust and integrity between parties to the evaluation) as the design unfolds, new data are found, new constructions are made, and new contingencies are faced by all parties.

4. Finally, fairness requires the constant use of the member-check process, defined earlier, which includes calls for comments on fairness, and which is utilized both during and after the inquiry process itself (in the data collection-analysis-construction stage and later when case studies are being developed). Vigilant and

assiduous use of member-checking should build confidence in individuals and groups and should lead to a pervasive judgment about the extent to which fairness exists.

Fairness as a criterion of adequacy for naturalistic evaluation is less ambiguous than the following four, and more is known about how to achieve it. It is not that this criterion is more easily achieved, merely that it has received more attention from a number of scholars (House, 1976; Lehne, 1978; Strike, 1982, see also Guba and Lincoln, 1985).

Ontological Authentication. If each person's reality is constructed and reconstructed as that person gains experience, interacts with others, and deals with the consequences of various personal actions and beliefs, an appropriate criterion to apply is that of improvement in the individual's (and group's) conscious experiencing of the world. What have sometimes been termed *false consciousness* (a neo-Marxian term) and *divided consciousnes* are part and parcel of this concept. The aim of some forms of disciplined inquiry, including evaluation (Lincoln and Guba, 1985b) ought to be to raise consciousness, or to unite divided consciousness, likely via some dialectical process, so that a person or persons (not to exclude the evaluator) can achieve a more sophisticated and enriched construction. In some instances, this aim will entail the realization (the "making real") of contextual shaping that has had the effect of political, cultural, or social impoverishment; in others, it will simply mean the increased appreciation of some set of complexities previously not appreciated at all, or appreciated only poorly.

Educative Authentication. It is not enough that the actors in some contexts achieve, individually, more sophisticated or mature constructions, or those that are more ontologically authentic. It is also essential that they come to appreciate (apprehend, discern, understand)—not necessarily like or agree with—the constructions that are made by others and to understand how those constructions are rooted in the different value systems of those others. In this process, it is not inconceivable that accommodations, whether political, strategic, value-based, or even just pragmatic, can be forged. But whether or not that happens is not at issue here; what the criterion of educative validity implies is increased understanding of (including possibly a sharing, or sympathy with) the whats and whys of various expressed constructions. Each stakeholder in the situation should have the opportunity to become educated about others of different persuasions (values and constructions), and hence to appreciate how different opinions, judgments, and actions are evoked. And among those stakeholders will be the evaluator, not only in the sense that he or she will emerge with "findings," recommendations, and an agenda for negotiation that are professionally interesting and fair but also that he or she will develop a more sophisticated and complex construction (an emic-etic blending) of both personal and professional (disciplinary-substantive) kinds.

How one knows whether or not educative authenticity has been reached by stakeholders is unclear. Indeed, in large-scale, multisite evaluations, it may not be possible for all—or even for more than a few—stakeholders to achieve more sophisticated constructions. But the techniques for ensuring that stakeholders do so even in small-scale evaluations are as yet undeveloped. At a minimum, however, the evaluator's responsibility ought to extend to ensuring that those persons who have been identified during the course of the evaluation as gatekeepers to various constituencies and stakeholding audiences ought to have the opportunity to be "educated" in the variety of perspectives and value systems that exist in a given context.

By virtue of the gatekeeping roles that they already occupy, gatekeepers have influence and access to members of stakeholding audiences. As such, they can act to increase the sophistication of their respective constituencies. The evaluator ought at least to make certain that those from whom he or she originally sought entrance are offered the chance to enhance their own understandings of the groups they represent. Various avenues for reporting (slide shows, filmstrips, oral narratives, and the like) should be explored for their profitability in increasing the consciousness of stakeholders, but at a minimum the stakeholders' representatives and gatekeepers should be involved in the educative process.

Catalytic Authentication. Reaching new constructions, achieving understandings that are enriching, and achieving fairness are still not enough. Inquiry, and evaluations in particular, must also facilitate and stimulate action. This form of authentication is sometimes known as feedback-action validity. It is a criterion that might be applied to conventional inquiries and evaluations as well; although if it were virtually all positivist social action, inquiries and evaluations would fail on it. The call for getting "theory into action"; the preoccupation in recent decades with "dissemination" at the national level; the creation and maintenance of federal laboratories, centers, and dissemination networks; the non-utilization of evaluations; the notable inaction subsequent to evaluations that is virtually a national scandal—all indicate that catalytic authentication has been singularly lacking. The naturalistic posture that involves all stakeholders from the start, that honors their inputs, that provides them with decision-making power in guiding the evaluation, that attempts to empower the powerless and give voice to the speechless, and that results in a collaborative effort holds more promise for eliminating such hoary distinctions as basic versus applied and theory versus practice.

Tactical Authenticity. Stimulation to action via catalytic authentication is in itself no assurance that the action taken will be effective, that is, will result in a desired change (or any change at all). The evaluation of inquiry requires other attributes to serve this latter goal. Chief among these is the matter of whether the evaluation is empowering or impoverishing, and to whom. The first step toward empowerment is taken by providing all persons at risk or with something at stake in the evaluation with the opportunity to control it as well (to move toward creating collaborative negotiation). It provides practice in the use of that power through the negotiation of construction, which is joint emic-etic elaboration. It goes without saying that if respondents are seen simply as "subjects" who must be "manipulated," channeled through "treatments," or even deceived in the interest of some higher "good" or "objective" truth, an evaluation or inquiry cannot possibly have tactical authenticity. Such a posture could only be justified from the bedrock of a realist ontology and an "objective," value-free epistemology.

Summary

All five of these authenticity criteria clearly require more detailed explication. Strategies or techniques for meeting and ensuring them largely remain to be devised. Nevertheless, they represent an attempt to meet a number of criticisms and problems associated with evaluation in general and naturalistic evaluation in particular. First, they address issues that have pervaded evaluation for two decades. As attempts to meet these enduring problems, they appear to be as useful as anything that has heretofore been suggested (in any formal or public sense).

Second, they are responsive to the demand that naturalistic inquiry or evaluation not rely simply on parallel technical criteria for ensuring reliability. While the set of additional authenticity criteria might not be the complete set, it does represent what might grow from naturalistic inquiry were one to ignore (or pretend not to know about) criteria based on the conventional paradigm. In that sense, authenticity criteria are part of an inductive, grounded, and creative process that springs from immersion with naturalistic ontology, epistemology, and methodology (and the concomitant attempts to put those axioms and procedures into practice).

Third, and finally, the criteria are suggestive of the ways in which new criteria might be developed; that is, they are addressed largely to ethical and ideological problems, problems that increasingly concern those involved in social action and in the schooling process. In that sense, they are confluent with an increasing awareness of the ideology-boundedness of public life and the enculturation processes that serve to empower some social groups and classes and to impoverish others. Thus, while at first appearing to be radical, they are nevertheless becoming mainstream. An invitation to join the fray is most cheerfully extended to all comers.

References

Guba, E. G. "Criteria for Assessing the Trustworthiness of Naturalistic Inquiries." *Educational Communication and Technology Journal*, 1981, *29*, 75-91.

Guba, E. G., and Lincoln, Y. S. "Do Inquiry Paradigms Imply Inquiry Methodologies?" In D. L. Fetterman (Ed.), *The Silent Scientific Revolution*. Beverly Hills, Calif.: Sage, in press.

84

Guba, E. G., and Lincoln, Y. S. *Effective Evaluation: Improving the Usefulness of Evaluation Results Through Responsive and Naturalistic Approaches.* San Francisco: Jossey-Bass, 1981.

Guba, E. G., and Lincoln, Y. S. "The Countenances of Fourth Generation Evaluation: Description, Judgment, and Negotiation." Paper presented at Evaluation Network annual meeting, Toronto, Canada, 1985.

House, E. R. "Justice in Evaluation." In G. V. Glass (Ed.), *Evaluation Studies Review Annual, no. 1.* Beverly Hills, Calif.: Sage, 1976.

Lehne, R. *The Quest for Justice: The Politics of School Finance Reform.* New York: Longman, 1978.

Lincoln, Y. S., and Guba, E. G. *Naturalistic Inquiry.* Beverly Hills, Calif.: Sage, 1985a.

Lincoln, Y. S., and Guba, E. G. "Ethics and Naturalistic Inquiry." Unpublished manuscript, University of Kansas, 1985b.

Morgan, G. *Beyond Method: Strategies for Social Research.* Beverly Hills, Calif.: Sage, 1983.

Strike, K. *Educational Policy and the Just Society.* Champaign: University of Illinois Press, 1982.

Yvonna S. Lincoln is associate professor of higher education in the Educational Policy and Administration Department, School of Education, the University of Kansas. Egon G. Guba is professor of educational inquiry methodology in the Department of Counseling and Educational Psychology, School of Education, Indiana University. They have jointly authored two books, Effective Evaluation *and* Naturalistic Inquiry, *which sketch the assumptional basis for naturalistic inquiry and its application to the evaluation arena. They have also collaborated with others on a third book,* Organizational Theory and Inquiry, *Sage, 1985.*

*Asking a few simple questions about the context of
an evaluation can help you decide if a naturalistic
approach is appropriate.*

When Is Naturalistic
Evaluation Appropriate?

David D. Williams

Should you use a naturalistic approach in your next evaluation? In this
chapter, conclusions drawn throughout the sourcebook are synthesized
through a practical aid to help evaluation designers and recipients (sponsors and clients) determine whether a naturalistic evaluation or a naturalistic component to a mixed-method study would best address their needs.
No single inquiry method will suffice for all evaluation needs. Ideally,
method is matched to the demands of the evaluation situation. It is better
to ask which method is most appropriate rather than how a familiar or
favorite method can be fit into a study (Patton, 1980).

To judge the usefulness of the naturalistic method for any given
evaluation circumstance, several questions about the situation should be
answered. The following sixteen questions, with sample answers regarding
a recent evaluation situation, are presented to determine the utility of the
naturalistic paradigm for a potential evaluation situation. Recently an
evaluation team at a university was asked by a neighboring school district
to evaluate a year-round education (YRE) program operating on a trial
basis at one school. The district and building administrators (the evaluation sponsors) wanted to know how effectively the program was being
implemented and what impact it was having.

1. Can most of the evaluation issues and criteria for making value

D. D. Williams (Ed.). *Naturalistic Evaluation.*
New Directions for Program Evaluation, no. 30. San Francisco: Jossey-Bass, June 1986.

judgments be clearly defined and operationalized before the study is initiated, or would it be helpful to explore the context and nature of the evaluand as part of the evaluation and allow issues and criteria to emerge during the study? If such exploration is desired, a naturalistic approach could help. Variables do not have to be operationalized in advance. Hypotheses do not need to be formulated in the evaluation proposal. The entire design remains flexible to maximize opportunities for exploration and better understanding of the variety of issues and multiple perspectives involved (Stake, 1975).

For the YRE study, several issues had already been defined by the building and district officials before the study ever began. Of course, these concerns had to be addressed, but the concept of year-round schools was new enough that these evaluation sponsors agreed that some effort to explore issues during the study was needed. Their interest in emerging as well as predefined evaluation issues suggested that a naturalistic component to the evaluation might be useful.

2. Are the official definitions of the evaluand held by the sponsors and evaluators (etic) and their value perspectives sufficient, or are the definitions and perspectives of participants (emic) such as persons responsible for various components of the evaluand also essential to the quality of the evaluation study? In the literature on naturalistic inquiry, the distinction between etic and emic perspectives highlights the importance of understanding and judging cultures, events, and concepts from the participants' emic or folk perspectives as well as from the inquirer's etic or theoretical point of view (Spindler, 1982). This acknowlegement of the value of a multiplicity of value perspectives could enhance almost any study.

The principal of the year-round school was both a sponsor and a participant in this study. He requested the evaluation and stated several official objectives early on. Later in the study, however, he was one of the persons in the school to be interviewed regarding his perspective from his central vantage point. In a sense then, the etic and emic perspectives were blended in this individual. But also, the views of parents and teachers on issues they defined, in addition to their response to concerns of the district administration, were requested by the sponsors. This interest in the emic as well as the etic perspective reinforced the need for a naturalistic study.

3. Is thick contextual description of the evaluand and its setting desired? If the evaluation consumers want qualitative portrayals, leading ideally to a vicarious experience of the evaluand as it functions naturally, then a naturalistic evaluation is essential. No other method could devote the time and intensity required to gather and report such rich detail (Geertz, 1973; Wolcott, 1975).

Although sponsors of the YRE were interested in how families were affected by the new schedule, what problems they encountered, and how the program worked at the school itself, they were less interested in the details of operation at the student and family level than a researcher would have been. Such detailed information would probably have helped them interpret the results and plan adaptations of the program in other schools; but they were unwilling to spend evaluation funds necessary to provide the reader of the report with a vicarious experience in a year-round school or in the family of a child in the school. Although the needs suggest the appropriateness of a naturalistic study, practical constraints prevent expenditures of resources that would be necessary to obtain thick contextual descriptions.

4. Would a formative evaluation be appropriate? Other methods are usually applicable; however the naturalistic paradigm is ideal for many formative evaluations because the design can be modified in response to new information needs (emerging issues again) as the study progresses and as the evaluand is improved. New questions can be asked without major revision of the evaluation plan because the evaluation is responsive to the variables defined as most critical by the participants and the setting. As a participant observer or quasi-participant in the situation under study, the evaluator can continually feed back evaluative information to the client.

For the YRE, there was a strong need for formative information. As the school and district were exploring the strengths and weaknesses of year-round schooling, the sponsors wanted feedback on what worked well and what to improve before expanding to other schools. Although not necessarily an indicator that a naturalistic approach was required (other methods provide formative evaluation data, too), the need for formative results suggested the possibility that a naturalistic evaluation would be useful.

5. Would a summative evaluation be appropriate? Although naturalistic evaluation is usually better suited to providing formative feedback (Bogdan and Biklen, 1982), it can be useful in understanding why an evaluand is or is not ultimately effective. If, in a summative evaluation, the client wants to know the details about what went right or wrong with the program or product, data collected naturalistically can be very helpful.

In the case of the YRE, formative rather than summative information was needed. Once the year-round concept has been formatively revised and improved, a summative evaluation might be requested. Then, if details about why the program is effective or not are requested, a naturalistic component may be included.

6. Is an evaluation of the processes by which the evaluand is addressing its outcomes needed? Naturalistic inquiry is particularly suited to process evaluation. Observation of the evaluand (or its related participants) in action by a naturalistic evaluator can reveal critical processes as they occur naturally. Interactions, relationships, strategies, and skills can be studied as they take place.

The sponsors of the YRE were interested in how the plan for year-round school was operationalized. They wanted to identify how parents used the new schedule, what teachers did differently and how the children behaved with three-week "vacations" interspersed throughout the year. Clearly, a naturalistic evaluation could help meet this objective.

7. Is an outcome evaluation needed? What is the nature of the outcome or product concerned? If there is interest in how good a product is or how valuable the outcome of a process is, naturalistic evaluation may be useful, depending on the nature of the outcome. If the outcome is an easily quantifiable one, such as performance on a written test or ratings on an attitude scale, other forms of evaluation could more efficiently collect that information. However, if the outcome includes complex actions in natural or real settings (such as teaching, learning, and family interaction), a naturalistic component within an evaluation would allow much richer descriptions and more dependable and credible value judgments.

Besides their interest in the processes involved in implementing the year-round school, sponsors wanted to know if participating students were learning more than before, if parents were more satisfied with the school, and whether the year-round school was more cost effective. Although descriptive details available through naturalistic evaluation about how students were learning and what parents and children were doing outside of school hours would help answer these questions, such a focus was considered of secondary importance by the sponsors of YRE.

8. Do evaluation recipients want judgments of the evaluand as it is operating in its natural state? Although tests and questionnaires can be natural components of an evaluand, they usually are not. It is often clear to the participants that completing evaluation instruments is not part of the normal activities associated with the program or product being evaluated. Naturalistic evaluations minimize data-gathering activities that interrupt the natural state of the evaluand by employing evaluators as participant observers who gather evaluative information informally over time while the evaluand is in natural operation.

Because the year-round school project had received public attention in the media, sponsors assumed that participants would expect to be asked about their reactions and would not perceive requests to grant interviews and complete questionnaires as unnatural. Although they hoped to study these reactions through observation as well as interviews, they also wanted quick feedback on participants' perceptions. Again, although the data from a naturalistic study were needed, practical constraints minimized the role naturalistic methods could play in the YRE.

9. Is there time to study the evaluand throughout its natural cycle (for example, an innovation in a school would best be studied during an entire school year)? A major strength of the naturalistic method is that variations within the evaluand can be investigated thoroughly over time (LeCompte and Goetz, 1982). If results are needed "immediately," qualitative interviews and some document analyses could be conducted (and such

variations on the naturalistic approach may be justified at times); but the true power of the method is dissipated because there is not enough time to observe the natural functions of the evaluand in their various forms.

Although the YRE sponsors were willing to fund a three-year study, they also wanted immediate feedback on problems and concerns of patrons and school personnel. They planned, too, to modify the program as they received feedback, making it difficult to study "a program" over the three-year period. So, although there was time for a naturalistic evaluation, the focus would have to be on the evolution of the year-round school program, and many intermediate feedback reports would need to be made throughout the study period.

10. In addition to the extensive time constraint listed above, does the situation permit intensive inquiry? To properly conduct naturalistic studies, the evaluators need to be on site regularly over time so they can become quasi-participants and gain the insiders' perspectives as they are naturally manifested. If the regular participants cannot permit such intense presence of the evaluators or if the evaluators do not have the resources to spend that much time, the quality of a naturalistic evaluation may suffer (Smith, 1979).

Although the sponsors of the YRE wanted the descriptive, formative, and process information naturalistic inquiry can provide, they would not allocate the funds needed to install participant observers in several classrooms and homes. Besides, it was not clear that teachers and families would permit that much intrusion. Again, naturalistic evaluation was wanted but not practical in its ideal form.

11. Can the evaluand be studied unobtrusively, as it operates naturally, in an ethical way? If the evaluand is not currently in operation, the evaluator may need to conduct a historical or an ex post facto study. If participant observations cannot be ethically made unobtrusively, more obvious modes of inquiry such as surveys and formal interviews should be used. Through hours of participation and informal interviews, naturalistic evaluators establish a rapport with participants that can make their presence commonplace and their purposes less obviously evaluative than may seem ethically appropriate. Precautions such as informed consent forms and member checks (Guba, 1981) of the data summaries will usually prevent unethical practices.

As stated earlier, although participant observers could have visited classrooms fairly unobtrusively (if the sponsors had been willing to budget for it), they could not have done so in homes of the participating students. Observers could have obtained permission to participate in family activities, but they would have needed much more time than the budget allowed to establish the trust and rapport necessary to gather useful information. Therefore, participant observation was not feasible for this study.

12. Are the evaluators qualified to be participant observers? Because

the inquirer is the principal instrument in a naturalistic evaluation, she or he must be well prepared and capable (Wolcott, 1975). Evaluators must be sensitive interviewers and perceptive observers; able to take rich field notes and to write well, aware of their own biases, willing to acknowledge their predispositions, and willing to study themselves as they study the evaluand to uncover the influence of their biases.

For the YRE study, a team of evaluators was available. Some members of the team specialized in measurement and experimental design; others had conducted naturalistic evaluations considered valuable by their consumers. Although they were not adequately aware of the qualities they should look for in a naturalistic evaluator, the sponsors were able to review earlier work done by members of this team as they made the decision to employ them. The qualifications of the team members made a naturalistic or a mixed-method evaluation possible in this case.

13. Do the evaluators and clients agree on a rational, justifiable, and comprehensible plan for analyzing the data? Procedures for analyzing and synthesizing qualitative data are not as well known as the graphic and statistical methods of quantitative analysis (Miles and Huberman, 1984). Clients should be confident that the evaluators will make sense of the data they collect naturalistically and will answer the evaluation questions clearly.

Although the evaluation team could have generated a plan for analyzing qualitative data, the sponsors of the YRE knew so little about naturalistic evaluation that they did not consider this question. The entire study would have been more successful if the sponsors and evaluators had discussed this issue before the study began, to clarify the evaluation questions and confirm that the analysis would address these issues. Although the evaluators could analyze the qualitative data, making a naturalistic study feasible, the evaluation could have been more successful if the clients had discussed the plan with them in advance.

14. Is triangulation of perspectives, data sources, and collection methods feasible? Naturalistic evaluators pursue any and all sources of information they can, assuming that confirmation of findings from disparate sources constitutes strong evidence. If clients or conditions associated with the evaluand were to prevent the evaluators from interviewing certain persons or reading certain documents, triangulation would be hindered and the quality of the evaluation would be seriously reduced (Guba, 1981).

In the case of the YRE, sponsors agreed that any and all data sources were available to the evaluation team. However, the size of the budget, the speed with which names of participating parents were provided, the processes used by the school to allow the evaluators to gather information from teachers, and the time constraints essentially prevented the team from tapping all those sources. Naturalistic evaluation was requested, but circumstances within the evaluation context prevented the degree of triangulation advocated by naturalistic inquiry theorists.

15. Are there resources and sufficient willingness to search for negative instances—for the evaluators to try to disprove their own evaluative conclusions, validate them, or at least seriously consider alternative interpretations of the results? Searching for instances in a data set that counter the pattern identified by the inquirer is a critical component of naturalistic evaluation. Because there is no experimental control of conditions, negative instance analysis is used to identify alternative explanations for the observed patterns. If the clients or the evaluators are not willing to critique their own work, the credibility of the study can be substantially weakened (Smith and Glass, forthcoming).

As stated earlier, the sponsors of the YRE were anxious to receive reports from the evaluation team as soon as possible. Therefore, although some verification through negative case analysis was possible in the analysis of existing data records, gathering of counterevidence was not planned during the first year of the evaluation. Perhaps during the second and third years, the evaluation team will have time to check their earlier conclusions with negative case analysis procedures. If they can, the evaluation will be more effective as a naturalistic study.

16. Is maintenance of an audit trail feasible? Because naturalistic inquiries are not easily critiqued through reviews of final reports alone, a complete record of the evaluation activities should be maintained and made available for public external meta-evaluation. This process does much to ensure the reliability of the study (Guba and Lincoln, 1981) although it requires time and effort. If the sponsors are unwilling to fund it or if the evaluators are unwilling to maintain the detailed records, the audit trail cannot be kept, and the value of the resulting evaluation is reduced (Miles and Huberman, 1984).

In the YRE, the sponsors did not request an audit or even that a trail be maintained. Because it was not funded and they suspected it would not be required, the evaluation team did not plan to maintain the necessary records, although they could have done so without much additional expense. Without an audit trail, the strength of a naturalistic evaluation is more easily challenged.

Summary

As shown by this analysis, many but not all the questions were answered affirmatively in the YRE case. In fact, a purely naturalistic evaluation was not appropriate in this situation, as is often the case (Williams, forthcoming). Rather, naturalistic methods were adapted (through lengthy in-depth interviews) and combined with more traditional quantitative approaches (surveys and testing) to address simultaneously and as appropriately as possible the most pressing concerns of the sponsors, the participants, and the evaluators. Likewise, the set of questions discussed here should help readers decide how, if at all, they should adopt or adapt the methods of naturalistic inquiry as they consider the characteristics of their evaluation circumstances.

References

Bogdan, R. C., and Biklen, S. K. *Qualitative Research for Education: An Introduction to Theory and Methods.* Boston: Allyn and Bacon, 1982.
Geertz, C. *The Interpretation of Cultures.* New York: Basic Books, 1973.
Guba, E. G. "Criteria for Assessing the Trustworthiness of Naturalistic Inquiries." *Educational Communication and Technology Journal,* 1981, *29,* 75-91.
Guba, E. G., and Lincoln, Y. S. *Effective Evaluation: Improving the Usefulness of Evaluation Results Through Responsive and Naturalistic Approaches.* San Francisco: Jossey-Bass, 1981.
LeCompte, M. D., and Goetz, J. P. "Problems of Reliability and Validity in Ethnographic Research." *Review of Educational Research,* 1982, *52* (1), 31-60.
Miles, M. B., and Huberman, A. M. *Qualitative Data Analysis.* Beverly Hills, Calif.: Sage, 1984.
Patton, M. Q. *Qualitative Evaluation Methods.* Beverly Hills, Calif.: Sage, 1980.
Smith, L. M. "An Evolving Logic of Participant Observation, Educational Ethnography, and Other Case Studies." *Review of Research in Education,* 1979, *6,* 316-377.
Smith, M. L., and Glass, G. V. *Research and Evaluation in Education and the Social Sciences.* Englewood Cliffs, N.J.: Prentice-Hall, forthcoming.
Spindler, G. (Ed.). *Doing the Ethnography of Schooling—Educational Anthropology in Action.* New York: Holt, Rinehart & Winston, 1982.
Stake, R. E. *Program Evaluation: Particularly Responsive Evaluation.* Occasional Paper no. 5. Kalamazoo: Western Michigan University Evaluation Center, 1975.
Williams, D. D. "Naturalistic Evaluation—Potential Conflict Between Evaluation Standards and Criteria for Conducting Naturalistic Inquiry." *Educational Evaluation and Policy Analysis,* forthcoming.
Wolcott, H. "Criteria for an Ethnographic Approach to Research in the Schools." *Human Organization,* 1975, *34,* 111-127.

David D. Williams is an assistant professor of curriculum and instructional science at Brigham Young University, in Provo, Utah, specializing in research on evaluation.

If one undertakes naturalistic evaluation without
formal training, there are some important
considerations and sources of information to
keep in mind.

On Your Own with Naturalistic Evaluation

Sari Knopp Biklen
Robert Bogdan

For many years educators interested in learning about naturalistic research methods apprenticed themselves to a social anthropologist or sociologist and learned the method from one of the "masters" as they conducted the study. While this process was fruitful for those few who were able to engage in it, the undersupply of masters could not meet the burgeoning demand of interest. Many researchers were forced to undertake dissertation or grant research without benefit of direct instruction. More recently, however, the number of courses as well as books published in qualitative methods has expanded, enabling training of greater numbers of interested people. In many locations, however, naturalistic methods courses are not offered, and interested parties must go it alone.

Naturalistic evaluation's reputation and appearance as "accessible" encourage would-be researchers to attempt projects employing these methods without having had any formal training. Indeed, participant observation (or ethnography) and in-depth interviewing are accessible because they rely on the skills of looking, listening, and speaking that we all employ daily. Accessibility is an attractive but somewhat deceptive feature of qualitative research. "Easy" to read does not necessarily mean easy to do. Students often report that from the outside, qualitative research meth-

D. D. Williams (Ed.). *Naturalistic Evaluation.*
New Directions for Program Evaluation, no. 30. San Francisco: Jossey-Bass, June 1986.

ods appear easier than they really are. Qualitative approaches, particularly participant observation, are labor intensive.

Instructional Literature

The literature on teaching qualitative research is really of three kinds. The first kind includes reports of direct teaching experiences, examples of which are collected in an excellent volume of *Anthropology and Education Quarterly* (1983). Here, many well-known qualitative researchers describe their methods for teaching fieldwork to educational researchers.

The second sort of instructional materials are books that literally instruct the reader in the methods of naturalistic research and articles that focus on some aspect or problem. The books may be intended for use in coursework or for the professional library. Those with a sociological bent include Bogdan and Biklen (1982) and McCall and Simmons (1969), a collection not directly related to educational evaluation, but which contains important discussions of issues from which naturalistic evaluators can benefit. Books rooted in an anthropological framework include Spindler (1982), Goetz and LeCompte (1984), and Guba and Lincoln (1981). Cassell (1978) is a fieldwork manual for studying desegregated schools, but the advice it contains can be effectively applied to other settings. Other instructional books not specifically rooted in education but containing good advice include Wax (1971), Agar (1980), Hammersley and Atkinson (1983), Becker (1970), and Burgess (1985). Fetterman (1984) pertains particularly to naturalistic evaluation methods.

The third kind of material instructs second-hand. This category includes qualitative researchers discussing the processes of fieldwork as they themselves have engaged in it. In these methodological autobiographies, researchers discuss the choices as well as the mistakes they made, taking the reader through stages of fieldwork step by step. The wide-ranging literature of this type includes some material specifically in education and some not, though it all discusses problems that researchers in most settings must face. Geer (1967), for example, discusses how her views changed in a study of higher education after a few weeks in the field. Bohannon (1981) takes the reader through the "natural" history of a research project. Wax (1971) describes the different stages of research projects as well as her mistakes when she studied Japanese relocation centers and when she and Wax studied native Americans. Everhart (1977) writes effectively of some of the tensions involved in long-term fieldwork in schools. Daniels (1983) takes the reader through several of her studies as she discusses self-deception and self-discovery in fieldwork. Metz (1983) and Wax (1979) discuss how researcher roles, as perceived by informants, shape the research act. Gans (1968) effectively describes the personal aspects of fieldwork that are also discussed in Shaffir, Stebbins, and Turowetz (1980), and Whyte (1984).

Naturalistic Assumptions

Some researchers who teach naturalistic methods teach the theoretical underpinnings for a whole semester before they let students go out into the field and gather data (Rist, 1983) while others encourage students to get their feet wet first (Bogdan, 1983). Whenever one learns a conceptual framework to support one's research, understanding naturalistic assumptions helps to explain the tenets of the qualitative approach to others who are not familiar with it. Anthropologists call on the framework of culture to ground their approach. For good descriptions, see Geertz (1973, 1983). Those with more affinity for sociology generally rely on symbolic interaction theory (see, for example, Bruyn, 1966; Blumer, 1969; Manis and Meltzer, 1967). These views emphasize the phenomenological nature and social construction of reality (Berger and Luckmann, 1967).

Naturalistic methods can be used in two ways. First, and less forcefully, they can be used as techniques in a study that has not been framed from a naturalistic perspective. Programs can be evaluated using observations or interviews to get at issues that have been determined previously. Studies of this type tend to be less inductive than those that use the first days in the field to discover which questions are important to the participants themselves. But they are more quickly carried out—a benefit to many evaluators. In this case, the evaluator applies naturalistic techniques to the situation, modifying the issues.

Second, the evaluator conceptualizes the study around what we call "thinking naturalistically." That is, the evaluator approaches reality as a multilayered, interactive, shared social experience that can be studied by first learning what participants consider important. In this case, the first days in the field are spent learning how participants think about and conceptualize issues (see Geer, 1967).

However the methods are used, they share some common threads when they are applied to the naturalistic evaluation. First, the researcher collects the data in the natural setting, and the researcher is the research instrument. Second, qualitative data are descriptive. They are soft, in narrative rather than statistical form. We call the data "rich" when they are filled with descriptions, conversations, and reporting of first-person experiences. Data that are filled with hearsay and overgeneralizations and that are lacking in specifics are weak.

Third, naturalistic evaluators focus on perspective. They study educational issues as they are perceived and experienced by people. Therefore, the evaluator must "translate" evaluation questions, as they are traditionally framed, to ones that fit the naturalistic mode. This mode only asks questions about perspective. The question, "Is individualized instruction successful at x--- School?" would be translated to "How do students experience individualized instruction at x--- School?"; "What do teachers mean by 'individualizing instruction'?" Research questions in the naturalistic mode get at the meanings people make of their experiences.

Finally, this method of analysis tends to be inductive. The researcher enters the field with some general questions in mind, but uses the first part of fieldwork to discover which questions are important in the particular context. As the evaluator spends time in the setting, the research focus narrows and the questions become more specific (see Whyte, 1984).

"Good Advice"

Earlier, we said that some materials describing the research process offer good advice to the reader. How does the novice distinguish between good and not-so-good advice? Or, how does the reader decide whose advice to take when advice is contradicting? In other words, when one has little direct experience with qualitative methods, how does one know what good advice is? How does one foresee potential problems? The only way to really evaluate the effectiveness of advice is to engage in fieldwork. There is no substitute for actual experience in this inquiry method. But experience blindly engaged in may not be helpful, so the literature discussed in the next section should provide some direction.

Nuts and Bolts of Naturalistic Evaluation

How do researchers monitor themselves as they carry out a qualitative evaluation? In this section we examine some of the major issues.

Field Relations. Because researcher and informants continually "rub shoulders" (Daniels, 1983), relating to informants becomes an important issue. Wax (1971) insists that good fieldworkers have luck and keep their wits about them. While in the setting, the fieldworker will probably have to engage in activities or conversations that create discomfort or anxiety. The ability to live with ambiguity and anxiety is an important resource to command.

When starting out, the fieldworker's first two primary tasks are getting in and establishing rapport. Getting by the gatekeepers can be more or less difficult, depending on the openness of the organization. Issues of how to gain access and deciding where to go for permission are discussed in terms of educational settings in Bogdan and Biklen (1982), Everhart (1975), and Goetz and LeCompte (1984), and in more general but also informative ways in Whyte (1984), Wax (1971), and Powdermaker (1966). Establishing rapport can be discussed in many ways. Everhart

(1977) describes what he calls "the three Rs" of fieldwork: role, reciprocity, and receptivity. Rapport building makes use of one's interpersonal skills and requires that the researcher make the informants feel comfortable and relaxed (see Botkin, 1945).

As a fieldworker, one coaches informants regarding how one wants to be seen by them. Everhart (1977) wanted the students he studied to know that he would not report them to their teachers. Rist (1978) helped teachers with their fears of the black students who were integrating the previously all-white school. Erikson (1976) had to learn which subjects were acceptable for casual discussion in an Appalachian community devastated by flood. Researchers talk about establishing field relations with different degrees of informality.

The evaluator has relationships not only with informants, from whom he or she hopes to learn, but with clients to whom he or she must present information as well. The evaluator must negotiate issues that could produce tension before beginning the research. If the client has experience with naturalistic evaluation, then these tensions are less apt to arise. The following concerns are among those that should be subjects of communication between the naturalistic evaluator and the client before beginning fieldwork:

1. Naturalistic evaluation can document and describe as well as assess. In this mode the process can be less threatening to those at the research site.

2. The client does not own the raw data of fieldnotes or interview transcripts. While the client may expect ownership, it would compromise the confidentiality that the evaluator must promise to informants in order to secure rich data. Confidentiality is difficult to maintain anyway at an evaluation site that cannot be anonymously represented.

3. Naturalistic evaluation studies problems in the social context in which they occur. Clients may worry when evaluators will not study a narrow problem isolated from all other programmatic concerns. This tension can be assuaged if it is discussed before fieldwork commences.

4. The naturalistic evaluator examines problems from the perspective of participants without regard to their position of power. Sometimes, clients react negatively to this approach if they expect the evaluator to accept the perspectives of those in power.

All these issues in relation to working with a client relate to two major issues. The first is that the evaluator works for someone, and that person holds a different perspective than the evaluator. And second, the client has certain expections about what evaluation should be and about what the outcomes will be. Early discussion can forestall problems and change expectations.

Other important issues to consider in field relations are presentation of self (Agar, 1980; Bogdan and Biklen, 1982), key informants, working on teams (Bogdan and Biklen, 1982; Everhart, 1975; Bohannon, 1981), and ethical issues (Cassell and Wax, 1980).

Data. Two factors are particularly important when thinking about data. First is the nature of data and what its different forms are. Second is the issue of what influences the data. Let us take these two issues in order.

In naturalistic evaluation data takes the form of fieldnotes. Whether the notes are from transcribed interviews, participant observations, career histories, or documents, the evaluator aims to have notes that are descriptive; that is, rich in details. A major worry of novice researchers is whether or not they will be able to remember what they see and hear. For advice on how to remember, see Bogdan and Biklen (1982), Hammersley and Atkinson (1983), and Agar (1980). Goetz and LeCompte (1984) have an excellent section on how to take advantage of life history methods in education. They emphasize the importance of the career history. Other sources for life history study include Plummer (1983) and Becker (1970). Certain methodologists focus more on interviewing, and others on observing. For observing, see Spradley (1980) and Berger (1972). For interviewing, see Douglas (1985), Ives (1974), Agar (1980), and Spradley (1979). Sources on both include Whyte (1984), Bogdan and Biklen (1982), and McCall and Simmons (1969). For a discussion of the ways in which some qualitative researchers think about quantitative data, see Bogdan and Ksander (1980) and Pelto and Pelto (1978).

The second issue to consider regarding data is what influences it. The naturalistic evaluator strives to avoid imposing alien meanings on what is seen and heard. When the researcher is the research instrument, he or she wonders how personal values influence what one chooses to see or to note. Fieldworkers keep a journal to document their reactions or to write memos on their personal feelings. It is also for this particular reason that qualitative researchers must collect data over an extended period of time. The large amount of data that the researcher collects makes the researcher's biases more fragile. The questions asked about these issues are numerous. How does the researcher know if the informant is telling the truth (Dean and Whyte, 1958)? How can one counteract bias in documents of life (Plummer, 1983)? Can one have strong values about an issue and still conduct inductive research (Thorne, 1983)? How do one's race, sex and age characteristics affect the quality of the data collected (Wax, 1979)?

Data Analysis. As in quantitative modes, the data in naturalistic evaluation have no meaning in themselves. They must be analyzed so that meaning is imposed on the data. For naturalistic evaluators the stages of the research project are not discrete. That is, design, data collection, and data analysis are not three different stages of the research process. Rather, they are intermingled. Because the design is inductive, for example, the design of the project continues after data are first collected as the researcher learns which issues are important to study.

Data analysis happens while data are being collected as well as after the evaluator has left the field. Data analysis is a process of making sense out of the data, finding out how the pieces fit together, what McCutcheon (1981) calls its "interdependence." The vehicles for analysis are memos and coding. Memos track one's thinking, make one attentive to process, and give one ideas to make data cohere. Since researchers analyze what is not said as well as what is said, memos enable them to note the unspoken while still in the field.

The first part of data analysis occurs while the evaluator is still taking notes. The evaluator tries to narrow the focus, moving from the broad opening questions to more specific ones. Memos help this narrowing-down process. Memos are written to cover a variety of issues including descriptions of informants; general discoveries; conceptual breakthroughs; emerging themes, thoughts, or worries; and methodological concerns (for examples of memos, see Bogdan and Biklen, 1982).

A second vehicle for data analysis is coding. The most difficult aspect of coding for most novices is the need to make judgments. For this reason we recommend a two-step process. First, read through notes, underlining issues that seem to be important, descriptive, or informative, writing notes on the wide left-hand margins. This is a good time to think about what material has been accumulated. Second, go back over the notes and sort the material into codes. There will probably be between forty and sixty major codes (Bogdan and Biklen, 1982). For an excellent discussion of the relationship of coding to grounded theory (Glaser and Strauss, 1967) see Charmaz (1983). Other helpful concepts include the domain analysis (Spradley, 1979, 1980) and typologies of awareness (Hammersley and Atkinson, 1983). Cassell (1978) includes a useful and practical discussion of organizing for coding. Whyte (1984) brings years of fieldwork experience to his discussion of data analysis.

Writing It Up. Some recent books on naturalistic research methods contain chapters on writing up the research (see, for example, Bogdan and Biklen, 1982; Hammersley and Atkinson, 1983). Two key issues relate to writing style. First, the contract report takes a different form from the publishable article. Federal or private agencies, as well as local education agencies, often dictate what to write and how to write it. They may want the report organized in a particular way. There is often less freedom in this situation. Second, because of the accessibility of qualitative data, it seems to us that the qualitative researcher has a special obligation to write up the data in an interesting and well-written manner. Perhaps in this area we can become leaders in the field.

Conclusion

Recent interest in naturalistic methods has resulted in a surge of publications. The evaluator who has less access to formal educational situations has many resources from which to draw. Also, more consultants in the field are available to help with particular problems.

100

References

Agar, M. *The Professional Stranger*. New York: Academic Press, 1980.

Anthropology and Education Quarterly, 1983, *14* (entire issue 3).

Becker, H. *Sociological Work*. Chicago: Aldine, 1970.

Berger, J. *Ways of Seeing*. London: Penguin, 1972.

Berger, P., and Luckmann, T. *The Social Construction of Reality*. New York: Doubleday, 1967.

Blumer, H. *Symbolic Interactionism*. Englewood Cliffs, N. J.: Prentice-Hall, 1969.

Bogdan, R. "Teaching Fieldwork to Educational Researchers." *Anthropology and Education Quarterly*, 1983, *14* (3), 171-177.

Bogdan, R., and Biklen, S. *Qualitative Research for Education: An Introduction to Theory and Methods*. Boston: Allyn and Bacon, 1982.

Bogdan, R., and Ksander, M. "Policy Data as a Social Process: A Qualitative Approach to Quantitative Data." *Human Organization*, 1980, *34* (4), 302-309.

Bohannon, P. "Unseen Community: The Natural History of a Research Project." In D. A. Messerschmidt (Ed.), *Anthropologists at Home in North America: Methods and Issues in the Study of One's Own Society*. Cambridge, England: Cambridge University Press, 1981.

Botkin, B. *Lay My Burden Down*. Chicago: Chicago University Press, 1945.

Bruyn, S. *The Human Perspective in Sociology*. Englewood Cliffs, N.J.: 1966.

Burgess, R. G. (Ed.). *Field Methods in the Study of Education*. London: Falmer Press, 1985.

Cassell, J. *A Field Manual for Studying Desegregated Schools*. Washington, D.C.: National Institute of Education, 1978.

Cassell, J., and Wax, M. (Eds.). *Ethical Problems in Fieldwork*. 1980, *27* (3), (Special issue of *Social Problems*).

Charmaz, K. "The Grounded Theory Method: An Explication and Interpretation." In R. M. Emerson (Ed.), *Contemporary Field Research*. Boston: Little, Brown, 1983.

Daniels, A. K. "Self-Deception and Self-Discovery in Fieldwork." *Qualitative Sociology*, 1983, *6* (3), 195-214.

Dean, J. P. and Whyte, W. F. "How Do You Know if the Informant is Telling the Truth?" *Human Organization*, 1958, *17*, 34-38.

Douglas, J. *Creative Interviewing*. Beverly Hills, Calif.: Sage, 1985.

Erikson, K. *Everything in Its Path*. New York: Simon and Schuster, 1976.

Everhart, R. "Problems of Doing Fieldwork in Educational Evaluation." *Human Organization*, 1975, *34*, (2), 205-215.

Everhart, R. "Between Stranger and Friend: Some Consequences of (Long Term) Fieldwork in Schools." *American Educational Research Journal*, 1977, *14* (1), 1-15.

Fetterman, D. (Ed.). *Ethnography in Educational Evaluation*. Beverly Hills, Calif.: Sage, 1984.

Gans, H. "The Participant-Observer as a Human Being: Observations on the Personal Aspects of Fieldwork." In H. Becker and others (Eds.), *Institute and the Person*. Chicago: Aldine, 1968.

Geer, B. "First Days in the Field." In P. Hammond (Ed.), *Sociologists at Work*. Garden City, N.Y.: Doubleday, 1967.

Geertz, C. "Thick Description: Toward an Interpretive Theory of Culture." In C. Geertz (Ed.), *The Interpretation of Cultures*. N.Y.: Basic Books, 1973.

Geertz, C. "From the Native's Point of View: On the Nature of Anthropological Understanding." In C. Geertz (Ed.), *Local Knowledge: Further Essays in Interpretive Anthropology*. N.Y.: Basic Books, 1983.

Glaser, B., and Strauss, A. *The Discovery of Grounded Theory*. Chicago: Aldine, 1967.

Goetz, J., and LeCompte, M. *Ethnography and Qualitative Design in Educational Research*. Orlando, Fla.: Academic Press, 1984.

Guba, E. G., and Lincoln, Y. S. *Effective Evaluation: Improving the Usefulness of Evaluation Results Through Responsive and Naturalistic Approaches*. San Francisco: Jossey-Bass, 1981.

Hammersley, M., and Atkinson, P. *Ethnography, Principles in Practice*. London: Tavistock, 1983.

Ives, E. *The Tape-Recorded Interview*. Knoxville: University of Tennessee Press, 1974.

McCall, G. J. and Simmons, J. L. (Eds.). *Issues in Participant Observation*. Reading, Mass.: Addison-Wesley, 1969.

McCutcheon, G. "On the Interpretations of Classroom Observations." *Educational Researcher*, 1981, *10* (5), 5-10.

Manis, J., and Meltzer, B. *Symbolic Interaction*. Boston: Allyn and Bacon, 1967.

Metz, M. "What Can Be Learned from Educational Ethnography?" *Urban Education*, 1983, *17* (4), 391-418.

Pelto, P., and Pelto, G. *Anthropological Research: The Structure of Inquiry*. (Second Ed.) Cambridge, England: Cambridge University Press, 1978.

Plummer, K. *Documents of Life*. London: Allen and Unwin, 1983.

Powdermaker, H. *Stranger and Friend: The Way of an Anthropologist*. New York: Norton, 1966.

Rist, R. *The Invisible Children*. Cambridge, Mass.: Harvard University Press, 1978.

Rist, R. "Transmitting the Craft of Qualitative Research." *Anthropology and Education Quarterly*, 1983, *14* (3), 202-205.

Shaffir, W., Stebbins, R., and Turowetz, A. (Eds.). *Fieldwork Experience*. New York: St. Martin's Press, 1980.

Spindler, G. (Ed.). *Doing the Ethnography of Schooling*. New York: Holt, Rinehart & Winston, 1982.

Spradley, J. *The Ethnographic Interview*. New York: Holt, Rinehart & Winston, 1979.

Spradley, J. *Participant Observation*. New York: Holt, Rinehart & Winston, 1980.

Thorne, B. "Political Activist as Participant Observer: Conflicts of Commitment in a Study of the Draft Resistance Movement of the 1960s." In R. Emerson (Ed.), *Contemporary Field Research*. Boston: Little, Brown, 1983.

Wax, R. *Doing Fieldwork*. Chicago: Chicago University Press, 1971.

Wax, R. "Gender and Age in Fieldwork and Fieldwork Education: No Good Thing is Done by Any Man Alone." *Social Problems*. 1979, *26*, 509-523.

Whyte, W. F. *Learning from the Field*. Beverly Hills, Calif.: Sage, 1984.

Sari Knopp Biklen is an associate professor in the department of cultural foundations of education.

Robert Bogdan is professor of special education and sociology. They are also affiliated with Syracuse University's Qualitative Research Center.

Index